COLUMBIA UNIVERSITY LECTURES
JULIUS BEER FOUNDATION

CANADA
AN AMERICAN NATION

CANADA
AN AMERICAN NATION

BY

JOHN W. DAFOE

NEW YORK: MORNINGSIDE HEIGHTS
COLUMBIA UNIVERSITY PRESS
1935

PRINTED IN THE UNITED STATES OF AMERICA
GEORGE BANTA PUBLISHING COMPANY, MENASHA, WISCONSIN

TO

JAMES T. SHOTWELL

A CITIZEN OF NORTH AMERICA WHOSE CAREER HAS CON-
FERRED DISTINCTION ON THE COUNTRY OF HIS BIRTH AND
THE COUNTRY OF HIS ADOPTION

PREFACE

WHEN HONORED by the invitation of Dr. Nicholas Murray Butler to deliver three lectures at Columbia University during the academic year 1933-34, I, as a Canadian journalist long interested in Canadian-American relations, thought the time and occasion opportune to discuss an aspect of these relations to which not enough consideration is given: the common foundation of early North American feeling and belief upon which the structures of government in both countries rest. The lectures are published as delivered at Columbia University, April 9, 11 and 13 of this year; but I have added a few footnotes and references in the hope that they may be of service to the reader.

J. W. DAFOE

WINNIPEG
DECEMBER, 1934

CONTENTS

I. CANADA'S RISE TO NATIONHOOD

II. CANADA AS A DEMOCRACY

III. CANADA AS NEIGHBOR

I

CANADA'S RISE TO NATIONHOOD

I

CANADA'S RISE TO NATIONHOOD

One of a Family of Free Nations

Two KINDRED nations divide the vast area of North America north of the Rio Grande. It is, with the possible exception of South America, the largest continuous territory in the world given over to a people, the great majority of whom derive from kindred sources —a people moreover who are subject to pressures, environmental, linguistic, social and commercial, which steadily strengthen their homogeneous elements. Of these pressures I put first that of language. The use of language is a discipline and an education in conformity in its large aspects. As a man speaks so he is. Bismarck is reported to have said that the greatest political fact of modern times was the "inherited and permanent fact that North America speaks English." The purpose of the British Empire, Cramb said, was to give all men within its bounds an English mind; and the statement is true if the words "an English mind" are not given a too narrow construction. The influences operating within the United States give an American mind, in whole or in part, to every resident; and the English mind and the American mind in their attitudes to fundamental political issues are not dis-

similar. In his book, *The English-Speaking Peoples,*
George L. Beer—whose premature death was a tragic
mishap to the cause of Anglo-American understanding—has something of moment to say on this point:

> In spite of the fact that the population of the United
> States is composed of many European strains, there is an
> essential unity in so far as the Caucasian native-born ele-
> ments are concerned. This unity of language has given
> to these Caucasians born in the United States a common
> mind and this mind does not differ in essentials from
> that of other English-speaking peoples. As has been said
> by Professor Hart "the standards, aspirations and moral
> and political ideals of the original English settlers not
> only dominate their own descendants but permeate the
> body of immigrants of other races." The son of the immi-
> grant into the United States finds himself at home in Can-
> ada, Australia or Britain while he feels himself a de-
> tached stranger within his own ancestral gates in con-
> tinental Europe.[1]

With the eye of imagination it is easy to see North
America as the stronghold of the English-speaking
world growing in power and numbers from century
to century.

The story of the growth of the American Union
from the Atlantic seaboard states to the mighty Republic of today is one of the great epics of democracy.
It is the story of a people who in obedience to an inner

[1] Beer, George Louis, *The English-Speaking Peoples, Their Future
Relations and Joint International Obligations;* New York, 1917, p. 190.

urge pushed their territory to the Pacific in something more than half a century, and then insured the greatness of the land by declaring at the cannon's mouth that the Union must forever endure. Your pride of national achievement, your high sense of destiny fulfilled, your faith in a future of steady advance to ever-rising levels, find ample justification in this record of achievement.

My purpose in coming before this audience is to speak to the best of my ability of the parallel development of the other North American nation—a story which differs from yours in many respects but in its own way has been, as it seems to us Canadians, as notable a manifestation as yours of the vision, courage and tenacity of North American democracy.

At this point a question may arise in the mind of some listener, to be put against my characterization of Canada as a "North American democracy." He may say, in keeping with what was not so long since a very common idea: "Canada is the colony of a European Empire: her North Americanism is little more than a geographical expression."

The central theme of this discussion of Canadian-American relations is the argument that what might be called North American ideas of government, of social obligations and of the institutions necessary to the functioning of a democracy have been exemplified by Canada, not obscurely in a small backward country but in a setting of world-wide range.

Canada is a North American nation. She is also one of a family of free nations which, in their prenational stage of existence, were integral parts of that Empire which was thus described by your orator, Webster, just a hundred years ago: ". . . a power which has dotted over the surface of the whole globe with her possessions and military posts, whose morning drumbeat, following the sun, and keeping company with the hours, circles the earth with one continuous and unbroken strain of the martial airs of England."[2] These younger British nations are not reproductions, as like as peas, of a majestic motherland. They are true national entities, the product of natural evolution and growth, with well-developed special characteristics and aptitudes.

A Commonwealth gathering of any kind, provided the national delegations to it are so chosen as to be truly representative, is the most striking demonstration that this world can furnish of the voluntary unity that can arise from wide diversities of view and temper where there is no element of subordination, but instead a disposition to find common ground in essentials. Political conferences such as the Imperial Conferences, which are now held at regular intervals, are least representative of the actual diversities and essential unities owing to the limitation imposed by the requirement of maintaining, in each delegation, a united political front. Beginning twenty-five years ago

[2] Daniel Webster, speech May 7, 1834.

there have been at intervals conferences of the press
of the Commonwealth in which all shades of Dominion opinion have been represented. All these conferences I have attended, being now, I think, the sole
working journalist of whom this can be said. Other
imperial gatherings representative of various interests
—educational, fraternal, religious, commercial—are
being constantly held. In all these meetings diverg-
ing national characteristics, variations in the rating
of values over a range of intangibles, diversity in instinctive attitudes of mind, reveal themselves naturally and inevitably; but this takes place within an environment of harmonious voluntary coöperation.

What I regard as the most significant of all these
Commonwealth gatherings was one which was held
last September in Toronto. It met with a minimum
of publicity; its meetings were held in private; there
has been restraint in the publication of the discussions and of the conclusions reached. Yet I note, particularly in Great Britain, constant reference to the
importance and significance of the meetings and of
the views that were there exchanged. This was the
British Commonwealth Relations Conference, which
assembled under the auspices of the Royal Institute
of International Affairs and its Canadian counterpart,
the Canadian Institute of International Affairs.[3] To
the calling of this conference there went two years of

[3] A Study of this conference has been published: *British Commonwealth Relations Conference*, ed. by A. J. Toynbee, London, Hum-
phey Milford, 1934.

study and preparation. "I wish," said a Canadian statesman, "that the official Imperial Conferences had preparation one-half as efficient and as complete as this unofficial gathering had received." The practical purpose of the conference was to consider the relations of the British nations under the conditions of today and to discuss the ways and means of practical coöperation.

The national delegations from each unit of the Commonwealth had been carefully chosen, not with the view to enabling them to speak with a single voice, but expressly for the purpose of bringing into the discussion all the diverse existing elements of opinion. In the Canadian delegation the whole range of political diversity was represented. At the left was Mr. Woodsworth, the leader of the Coöperative Commonwealth Federation, Canada's newly organized and potentially formidable Socialist Party. At the other end of the scale there were champions of a conception of imperial relationships which belongs to yesterday. Political parties in all the British nations were represented by public men of distinction, but no one actually a member of a government or holding an official position was regarded as eligible, it being known that the holding of office inhibits the free expression of individual opinion.

The discussions which took place during the ten days of the conference were, to my way of thinking, of high interest and significance. The realities of today with respect to the working relationships of the British nations and, of still more profound importance, the relations that are practicable between the British nations, individually and collectively, and the outside world, were presented to the conference, in the first instance by Canadian speakers, with a vigor and directness which determined the course and the character of the discussions. There were three main schools of thought in the membership of the conference. There were those who sighed over the vanished Empire. There were those who desired the Commonwealth to consolidate itself anew on lines of economic exclusiveness and military preparedness, into a formidable combination which would play a leading part in the world drama of tomorrow. And there was the view that such a consolidation would add nothing to the security of its members, but rather would put them in jeopardy; that the Commonwealth must remain a family of free nations subject to two limitations upon their sovereignty: that which they voluntarily concede to that spirit of friendly coöperation which is seemly in a family; and externally, the subordination of foreign policy to their engagement to act collectively with other nations in establishing and enforcing peace.[4] This conception of nationalism, tempered by moral domestic considerations and by obligations, express and implied, to the world at large, was Canadian in its origin and in the manner of its

[4] For an interesting comment on the international aspects of the Conference discussions see *The Drift Towards War* in the *Yale Review*, 1934, by Philip Noel Baker, a member of the Conference.

presentation to the Commonwealth Relations Conference. It at once enlisted support from influential members of the delegations from Great Britain and South Africa; and, as the discussion went forward, it could be observed that it more and more commended itself to the judgment of the conference. Many of those to whom this policy was obviously distasteful on grounds of emotion and sentiment gave their intellectual adhesion to it as showing the only available road to a future that would protect the Commonwealth against strains that might destroy it.

The Political Inheritance of Canada

I could not but think as I noted these proceedings that here we had, on a small scale, an example of the processes by which Canadians achieved nationhood for themselves and at the same time profoundly modified the structure of the British Empire. The empire of central authority and obedient provinces is gone; and the influence that transformed it flowed largely from a circumstance whose significance, obscured for many decades, we can now in retrospect appraise. That circumstance was that the principle upon which that empire was built was repugnant to the populations of its colonies in British North America which made up the bulk of its colonial possessions. This repugnance was due to the fact that these colonies in their political inheritance were North American and wholly democratic. They had a political instinct which rejected the theory of government upon which the Empire was founded; and once the initial economic pressures which dulled this instinct were relaxed, there began a movement for modifications in the imperial scheme, as affecting these colonies, which, because it had in it the germ of the doctrine of equality, made the breakdown of the Imperial theory, given time, inevitable; because the modifications made in response to Canadian pressure extended of necessity to the whole Empire.

Speaking some four years ago to an audience in London, I said that many of the misconceptions which Englishmen visiting Canada acquired, arose from their inability to realize that Canada was an American country. I went on to say:

Canada is an American country by virtue of a common ancestry with the people of the United States. When one talks of a common ancestry between Canadians and Americans, people say "Yes, they had a common ancestry in England." But it is something closer than that. The common ancestry to which I refer occupied the American colonies prior to the Revolution. The English-speaking provinces in Canada were settled by citizens of the English colonies along the Atlantic sea-board. The generations which laid the cultural foundations of Canada and their forbears had lived in those colonies for a hundred or a hundred and fifty years—four or five generations. They had lived divorced from English influences, thrown very largely upon their own resources, and faced with problems upon which the experience of England threw no light.

Along the Atlantic coast, cut off from people with the aristocratic point of view, they developed an indigenous American civilization, now the common inheritance of Canada and the United States. The difference between the Americans who came into Canada after the War of Independence and the Americans who stayed at home was not profound. The people who were driven into exile were called Tories by the Americans, but that term was true of only a very small element. The great bulk of these people were of precisely the same type as the men in the American armies, but they did not think that the situation which had arisen between the colonies and Great Britain was one which could be profitably settled by an appeal to the sword. They thought that by patience and steady resort to constitutional methods the difficulties could be adjusted.[5]

Let me enlarge upon this, for it is the very fiber of my thesis. In discussing the question of the constitutional development of the Empire, the terms "First Empire," "Second Empire," and "Third Empire" (which is the Commonwealth) are commonly employed. Pundits rage against the distinctions but, as is usually the case with pundits, they are wrong.[6] Now, the principles which, if observed, would have kept

[5] *Journal of the Royal Institute of International Affairs,* London, Nov. 1930.
[6] Dr. Alfred Zimmern chose the title *The Third British Empire* for his book embodying a series of lectures delivered at Columbia University under the auspices of the Julius Beer Foundation (New York, 1926).

the First Empire intact and the English race one and indivisible, are precisely the principles upon which the present Commonwealth is founded. In the Second Empire we see a determined and persistent effort to replace these principles, which were rooted in democratic instinct and tradition, with principles in essence aristocratic and imperialistic; and it took just about a century and a half for the original conception of Empire relationships—which was American in origin —to overtake and push aside the bastard idea of centralization and control which destroyed the First Empire and would have as surely destroyed the Second, had it not been challenged.

"The Greek colonies," said Goldwin Smith, "took nothing from the mother countries but the sacred fire and freedom." The sacred fire that the English colonists carried with them, when they braved the North Atlantic in their cockleshells, was the rudimentary conception of self-government by means of elective assemblies. But the development of the idea did not proceed in the homeland and in the over-sea colonies on parallel lines or at the same pace. By the American assemblies practically the whole adult male population was admitted to a share in the government through their control of the purse. This was possible because intrenched privilege and vested interests were not strong enough to slow up this democratic development. But in England oligarchics and class combinations continued in easy charge of the governmental controls until a time within the memory of living men. For two centuries or more there was no general admission of the people to the franchise; and, after these conditions were modified, the social authority of these classes kept their political authority intact. Bagehot in his *English Constitution* has an enlightening word upon the deferential organization of British society, in both its social and political manifestations.

There appears to have been no understanding in Great Britain of the extent to which democratic self-government had developed in the colonies until the taxation policies of the British government were challenged. We get a contemporary expression of the alarm and chagrin to which this revelation of democratic American insubordination gave rise in a letter written by Sir Guy Carleton, Governor of the newly conquered Province of Quebec in January, 1768, to his official superior, the Earl of Shelburne. The English-speaking residents of Quebec who had gone into the Province of Quebec largely from the Atlantic colonies, demanded an assembly; and in his letter Carleton set out the reasons why, in his judgment, it should not be granted. He wrote:

It may not be improper here to observe that the British form of government, transplanted into this continent never will produce the same fruits as at home, chiefly because it is impossible for the dignity of the Throne and Peerage to be represented in the American forests. . . . A popular assembly which preserves its full vigour and in a country where all men appear nearly upon a level must give a strong bias to Republican principles.[7]

That opinion was inspired by a disturbance in Sir Guy's mind occasioned by his observation of events in the thirteen colonies. Already he was formulating in his mind means by which he could throw the weight of the conquered province into the scale against the English colonies; the harvest of his thoughts and plans was the enactment six years later of the Quebec Act which, as the Declaration of Independence clearly states, was one of the occurrences which precipitated the Revolution. Carleton did not want his project interfered with by a "popular assembly" with its tendency, in the absence of the restraining influence of an upper class, to encourage what he regarded as republican ideas. Then and for long afterward in the official mind and in official language, democracy, if the real article, was a term interchangeable with republicanism.

A quaint expression of the view universally held in official circles that the Revolution was the result of a usurpation of power by the popular assemblies is to be found in a letter written in 1790 by William Smith, Chief Justice of Quebec, to the governor, Lord Dorchester (Guy Carleton), embodying suggestions about the Constitutional Act then being drafted. Smith, who was an exile from New York, where

[7] Kennedy, W. P. M., *Documents of the Canadian Constitution, 1759-1915*, Toronto, 1918.

formerly he had held high office, wrote feelingly:

My Lord, an American Assembly, quiet in the weakness of their Infancy, could not but discover in their Elevation to Prosperity that themselves were the substance and the Governor and Board of Council mere shadows in the Political Frame. All America was thus, at the very outset of the Plantations, abandoned to Democracy.[8]

In my next quotations I jump forward some seventy-five years to show you that in 1863 fear and distrust of democratic assemblies in the colonies still dominated the minds of the class that governed Great Britain. My authority is not official, but it will serve, as it is from the *Times* which then, as always, perfectly reflected the views, antipathies and hopes of the more moderate elements of the governing class. My quotations are from an article in which in 1861 the *Times* thundered against the excesses, as it judged them, of democratic self-government in Australia. Said the *Times:*

It is evident that the balance of society and of government in these communities has been overthrown and that they are now governed by a single class, and that class the most ignorant and the least respectable of all. . . . There is no limit to this downward tendency; there is no power in the single class which governs these communities to regenerate itself. In an evil hour the Colonial Assemblies were entrusted with the power of reducing at their will the qualification of electors. . . . We ought never to

[8] Idem., p. 191.

have given them universal suffrage unless we intended to adopt universal suffrage ourselves.

It urged the imperial government to intervene by veto or by parliamentary action. Was Parliament—it asked—to allow this state of things to go on?

I find this quotation in *The Empire,* a collection of letters written to the London *Daily News* in 1862 by Goldwin Smith. He buttresses the language of the *Times* by an extract from a speech by the Duke of Newcastle, Secretary of State for the Colonies. The Duke remarks that he wishes the Australian colonies had been less precipitate in applying manhood suffrage. Australia is a "country where those established rights and interests were not to be found which might prove a check to it in other countries."

Goldwin Smith in these letters, noting the contrasts in government between Great Britain and the colonies, remarked:

"England is an aristocracy while the whole frame of Society to which political institutions must conform, is in Canada democratic."

If this was the contrast in 1862 between government at "home" and in colonies overseas, how much more marked was the difference in 1776! The clash which ended in the American Revolution was between an aristocratic government functioning through a parliament which was a perfect instrument for its will, and the elective assemblies of the American colonies which were outright democratic institutions. These assemblies had been set up promptly in every colony at the demand of the colonists and their power had grown because there was no counter-power to say them nay. They were regarded by the colonists as essential to their welfare.

Nova Scotia, the fourteenth American colony, erected on territory wrested from the French, was set going about the middle of the eighteenth century by the establishment of a military capital at Halifax. But the settlers who gave substance to the colony came from the New England colonies. They found themselves under the rule of officials attached to the governor's staff. To this they at once offered vigorous opposition, and their demand for an assembly was pressed upon the home authorities by Chief Justice Belcher, who was himself from Massachusetts. The military governor offered a stout resistance. An assembly, he said, would "serve only to create heats, animosities and disunion among the people."[9] After four years of agitation the Assembly was established. As the events of the next few years were to show, the people of Nova Scotia were more compliant than the inhabitants of the other colonies with the taxation policies of the British government, but even they would not submit to the rule of officialdom.

There could not thus be common ground between the Parliament of Great Britain and the Assemblies

[9] Martin, Chester, *Empire & Commonwealth; Studies in Governance and Self-Government in Canada*, Oxford, The Clarendon Press, 1929, pp. 68-69.

of the colonies, once the dispute arose; they were on different planes of political development. They were contemporary only in the technical sense of time; one party to the dispute was an oligarchy with medieval ideas about government; in the other the doctrines of modern democracy, revolutionary for those times, were astir. It was impossible for the older body, with its historic roots, its prestige, its sense of power and authority, even to begin to understand the political language of the colonies. Not even the friends of America in the motherland could grasp the American contention that their Assemblies were outside the jurisdiction of the British Parliament and subject only to the prerogative of the monarch.

The terms upon which the American Revolution could have been forestalled are a matter of record. Looked at in the light of today, the concessions were trivial, put in the balance against the disruption of an empire; but we must look in the history of the constitutional development of Canada to find a measure for the width and the depth of the gulf which separated the demands of the colonists and the convictions of George the Third and his advisers (perhaps it would be more accurate to say his assistants) as to the only workable polity of empire.

Parallels with Pre-Revolutionary America

There are three statements associated with the American Revolution which have parallels in the

Canadian record; and when the dates are compared an idea can be got of how impossible it was for British statesmanship in the seventies of the eighteenth century to understand and still less to act upon the propositions put forward by the colonists.

The first is article four of the Declaration of the First Continental Congress in 1774 as drafted by John Adams: Here the claim was made that the colonists "are entitled to a free and exclusive power of legislation in their several provincial legislatures, subject only to the negative of their sovereign in such manner as has been heretofore used and accustomed." But the right of the British Parliament to regulate the external trade of the colonies "for the purpose of securing the commercial advantages of the whole empire to the Mother country" was conceded.[10]

It was not until 1839, more than half a century later, that it occurred to a British statesman that the division of power between the Imperial and the Colonial Parliaments suggested by Adams in 1774 might afford a solution for the imperial problem of that day. Lord Durham in his report proposed self-government for the Canadian colonies, to be accompanied by the "perfect subordination" of the colonies to the British government with respect to all external matters.

The exception, had there been a settlement in 1774 on these terms, would doubtless have proved as un-

[10] The full text of article four is given in *The American Revolution: A Constitutional Interpretation,* by C. H. McIlwain, New York, 1923, p. 115.

workable in the American colonies as it afterwards proved in Canada. Of Lord Durham's reservation in the case of Canada, in the light of its subsequent abandonment, Sir C. P. Lucas has said: "He did not seem fully to recognize that when once an overseas community has been endowed with national institutions it is difficult, if not impossible, to set limits to its growth as a nation or permanently to withhold any subject as outside its scope."

The most comprehensively succinct statement of the issue between the British Parliament and the first American colonies was that made by Madison. He wrote in 1800:

The fundamental principle of the revolution was that the Colonies were co-ordinate members with each other and with Great Britain, of an Empire united by a common executive sovereign. The legislative power was maintained to be as complete in each American parliament as in the British parliament. And the Royal Prerogative was in force in each colony by virtue of its acknowledging the King for its executive magistrate as it was in Great Britain by virtue of a like acknowledgment there. A denial of these principles by Great Britain and the assertion of them by America produced the revolution.[11]

It was not until 1926—150 years after this issue was put, in the old colonies, to the test of the sword—that

[11] *The Writings of James Madison,* ed. by Gaillard Hunt, New York, Putnam, 1910, VI, 373. Also Robt. L. Schuyler, *Parliament and the British Empire,* New York, Columbia University Press, 1929, pp. 196-97.

the principle thus defined by Madison was accepted as the true basis of empire with the consent of Great Britain, which thus renounced its position of central authority. The parallel between Madison's statement and the governing affirmation of the Balfour declaration in 1926 is exact. Of the "group of self-governing communities composed of Great Britain and the Dominions" the declaration said:

Their position and mutual relation may be readily defined. They are autonomous communities within the British Empire, equal in status, in no way subordinate one to another in any aspect of their domestic or external affairs, though united by a common allegiance to the Crown and freely associated as members of the British Commonwealth of Nations.[12]

Let me now quote a statement in which the Centralist argument against the demand of the colonies was put in some twenty words. Governor Hutchinson, speaking to the Massachusetts Assembly in January, 1773, said: "I know of no line that can be drawn between the supreme authority of Parliament and the total independence of the Colonies."[13]

In the long contest in Canada for responsible government the argument of Hutchinson was repeated, until it became a commonplace, as the supposedly conclusive answer to the case put forward by the reformers.

[12] *Imperial Conference. 1926. Summary of Proceedings.* Cmd. 2768, p. 14. Kennedy's *Documents of the Canadian Constitution*, p. 703.
[13] Quoted in McIlwain's *American Revolution*, p. 123.

In the few uncompromising words of Hutchinson we find the explanation of why force alone could break the deadlock between the American colonies and the government in London.

Professor W. B. Munro of Harvard—one of the many Canadians who have found their talents acceptable to American universities and have repaid the opportunity given them by conspicuously brilliant service—says of Madison's principle that it "would probably have gained full recognition at Westminster a whole century or more ago if the American Revolution had not occurred."[14] But the Revolution could not be avoided because the Americans could not accept subordination and Great Britain would not permit them to stay in the Empire on any other condition; nor was it then possible for the idea of peaceful separation to rise in the minds of men.

Therefore the issue moved with all the inevitability of Greek tragedy through the arena of discussion to the battlefields. It was a clash of opposing principles that could not be adjusted within the ambit of a single political system.

Democratic vs. Aristocratic Conceptions of Government

The movement for nationhood in Canada began when in the new British colonies the settlers from the older American colonies, who had been driven into

[14] Munro, W. B., *American Influences on Canadian Government,* Toronto, 1929, p. 48.

exile by the victors, sought to reproduce the customs
and the institutions with which they were familiar;
and it closed when the principle of coördinate membership, so clearly set forth by Madison, was finally
established. In time it covered a century and a half.
In its humble beginnings it was instinctive and un-
knowing. The people of Canada were far on the road
before they understood whither they were bound.
Those who resisted and fought the movement realized what it meant; but they fought against the stars
since it was no more possible for Canada, once it had
attained a measure of power, to remain subordinate to
an overseas authority than it was for the American
colonists in the eighteenth century.

A very common observation, at least in Canada,
forty or fifty years ago, was that Great Britain learned
the art of governing colonies from the disaster of the
American Revolution. The statement is inexact. What
the British government drew from the loss of the
colonies, as Professor H. E. Egerton says, was the moral
"that democratic institutions are a menace to the
Mother country and should therefore if possible be
avoided."[15] When Great Britain began to build up a
second colonial Empire on the North American continent, the authorities were of one mind that the
mistakes (as they regarded them) which had attended

[15] Egerton, H. E., *The Origin & Growth of the English Colonies
and of Their System of Government; An Introduction to Mr. C. P.
Lucas's Historical Geography of the British Colonies,* Oxford, The
Clarendon Press, 1903, p. 16.

the founding of the earlier colonies must not be repeated. The new colonies were not to be abandoned, in the words of Chief Justice Smith, to the fatal spirit of democracy.

At the close of the Revolutionary War Great Britain retained two of her North American colonies—Canada (or to give it its official name, Quebec), a French province, and Nova Scotia (soon to be divided into two provinces, Nova Scotia and New Brunswick).

Here the loyalists, fleeing from the triumphant American states, found refuge. One estimate is that 35,000 loyalists went to Nova Scotia, and 20,000 to Quebec, more than half of them going from the province of New York. The New England migration was directed, in its entirety, to Nova Scotia. It dowered that province with scholars, jurists, men of affairs, clergymen of note, who became the leaders of the community. Since there is an intellectual fervor for reaction, as there is for revolution, there were, for a somewhat lengthy period of time, fewer signs in that province than in Canada of the coming to life of the North American spirit of democracy; yet when the revival came, such was the vigor and effectiveness of the movement, such the competence of the leadership, that responsible government, the road to nationhood, was achieved with promptitude and without the convulsions which marked its attainment in Canada.

It is in the history of Canada that we see most clearly the origins and the development of the struggle be-

tween the democratic conception of government that
was carried there from the English colonies along the
Atlantic, and the imported and imposed scheme of
government which the British statesmen of the day
regarded as the embodiment of the lesson taught by
the Revolution. There is a wealth of documentary
material available in the letters which passed back and
forth between the parties who were planning the new
arrangements made necessary by the influx of the
Loyalists.

These refugees came into a territory which had already been supplied by the Quebec Act with a carefully thought out scheme of government. The first
effect of the impact of the American influx was the
recognition that the Quebec Act would not do for
the districts in which the Loyalists were finding
homes, and that it would have to be modified in essential respects in the areas occupied by the French-
speaking subjects. Hence the deliberations and interchanges of views preceding the enactment of the Constitutional Act of 1791. By this Act the Province of
Quebec, as it had been constituted seventeen years
before, was divided into the provinces of Upper and
Lower Canada. The latter included the French towns
and settlements, the former the relatively unsettled
areas along the Great Lakes and the upper St. Lawrence, into which the Loyalist inflow had been directed. A legislative assembly, which had been denied
by the Quebec Act, was conceded to both provinces;

but exceeding care was taken that these assemblies should resemble only in name the bodies in the colonies that had delivered those communities to democracy. While the Act was in the making Grenville, the Home Secretary, wrote to Lord Dorchester, the Governor of Canada, that the Crown must have a "certain and improving revenue" from sources "beyond legislative control."[16] If this, he said, had been the rule in the older colonies it "would have retained them to this hour in obedience and loyalty." An appointed legislative council, made up of a specially created nobility with hereditary titles, was outlined as desirable. There would be thus supplied "A body of men having that motive of attachment to the existing form of government which arises from the possession of personal or hereditary distinction," to act as a buffer against change.

We find an almost complete picture of the ideal colony in the British style in the writings public and private of John G. Simcoe, the first Lieutenant Governor of Upper Canada. Simcoe as subaltern was at Bunker Hill; among the troops that surrendered at Yorktown was the light cavalry regiment, the Queen's Rangers recruited in Connecticut, which he commanded. The intervening years had been marked for him by much fighting and many wounds, and he returned to Great Britain after the war, still in his

[16] Kennedy's *Documents of the Canadian Constitution*, 2d. ed., pp. 199 ff.

twenties, with a reputation for devotion to the lost cause that brought him high praise from George III, and with a lively dislike for the victors in the struggle. His Canadian biographer speaks of "his blind fidelity to the King's Cause." When the project of dividing Quebec took shape he was advised that he would be given charge of Upper Canada; and in the light of this knowledge he wrote to a friend in January, 1791, giving in outline some of his hopes for the new province. Simcoe could not bring himself to believe that the separation of the English race was permanent. The outcome of the Revolution and the establishment of the Republic was to him some kind of horrid dream that would pass away. He hoped that the establishment of a model government, new colonial style, in the forests of Upper Canada would in some way contribute to this end.

I mean to prepare for whatever Convulsions may happen in the United States and the Method I propose is by establishing a free honorable British Government and a pure administration of its Laws which shall hold out to the solitary Emigrant, and to the several States, advantages that the present form of Government doth not and cannot permit them to enjoy. There are inherent Defects in the Congressional form of Government; the absolute prohibition of an order of nobility is one.[17]

[17] *The Correspondence of Lieut. Governor John Graves Simcoe, with Allied Documents Relating to His Administration of the Government of Upper Canada.* Collected and edited by Brigadier General E. A. Cruikshank . . . for the Historical Society, Ontario, 1923-31, pp. 17-18. Hereafter referred to as the *Simcoe Papers.*

The fervency of Simcoe's desire to see the lost colonies recovered thus found expression: "I would die by more than Indian torture to restore my King and his Family their just inheritance and to give my Country that fair and natural accession of Power which an Union with their Brethren could not fail to bestow and render permanent." The value of the reunion, it will be noted, is expressed in terms of military power. In the new province there was to be, Simcoe hoped, "a hereditary Council with some mark of Nobility." He would have a bishop, by which he meant that the Church of England would be established and endowed. There would be an English chief justice. The colony was to be the home of the arts and sciences. "This colony" he said, "should in its very Foundations provide for every Assistance that can possibly be procured for the Arts and Sciences and for every Embellishment that may hereafter Decorate and attract Notice, and may point it out to the Neighboring States as a Superior, more happy and more polished form of Government."

The same note of cheerful appreciation of the superiority of the new system was sounded when the Constitutional Act was submitted to Parliament a few months later. Parliament, Lord Grenville said, was "about to communicate the blessings of the English Constitution to the subjects of Canada because they were fully convinced that it was the best in the world." The supreme virtue of the Constitution, it was explained, was found in its happy combination of the aristocratic and the democratic elements. In the American colonies unbridled democracy had run wild without the counterweight of a House of Lords; while the authority of the Crown had lacked the support of a hereditary aristocracy and an established church. These errors, it was declared, were to be guarded against in the new colonies. By the scheme thus adopted the actual power was vested in the governor; an executive council, appointed by the British government, was to advise and assist him; there was to be a legislative council of life members to whom hereditary titles carrying right of membership in the Upper House would be issued if conditions permitted; and a legislative Assembly, elected on a wide franchise but with such limitation of control over the collection and distribution of revenue as to deprive it almost completely of the power of the purse. A reserve of land, equal to one-seventh of all land granted, was set aside as an endowment for a "Protestant clergy," which term was interpreted for many decades as meaning only the clergy of the Church of England.

John G. Simcoe, as a Member of Parliament, assisted in the passage of the Constitutional Act and thereafter set sail for Canada to bring his model colony into being. All the circumstances favored him. There were no encumbrances or handicaps; the field was clear for constructive experiments. The colony was remote from the great world. Its peoples were, to a man, British by blood or by inclination, tested by war and sacrifice. They were insulated against influences from the new Republic by the resentments, hatreds, and grievances of a fratricidal war. But in spite of these seemingly favorable conditions, Simcoe's achievements fell far short of his hopes; many of his plans miscarried; others in their practical application bore little resemblance to the dreams he had dreamed in England. In a letter to the Duke of Portland, written toward the end of his term, he said: "I have endeavoured to establish the form as well as the spirit of the British Constitution by modelling all the minutest branches of the Executive Government after a similar system and by aiming as far as possible to turn the views of His Majesty's subjects from any attention to the various modes and customs of the several provinces from which they emigrated, to the contemplation of Great Britain itself, as the sole and primary object of general and particular imitation."[18]

Governor Simcoe in this attempted the impossible and was paid for his temerity in disappointment. The settlers had brought from their American homes a desire to continue in their new homes the "modes and customs" to which the governor objected; they wanted to reproduce the simple municipal methods of the old colonies; their views about schools were not those of the governor; they, by a very large majority, preferred the ministrations of itinerant dissenting minis-

[18] Simcoe to Portland, Jan. 22, 1795, *Simcoe Papers*, p. 265.

ters—"sectaries" Simcoe called them—to the services of the Church of England, which was regarded by the Governor as a sure bulwark for the Constitution. Owing to the poverty of the people, the scheme for creating a nobility had to be postponed (forever, fortunately); his plan to have lieutenants appointed for the counties was regarded with such dislike that it did not long survive his departure; his proposal to turn the towns over to corporations so organized that the elections would be "as little popular as possible, meaning such corporations to tend to the support of the Aristocracy of the Country" was rejected as quixotic by the home authorities. One of Simcoe's earliest disappointments wears a comic air. The settlers chose, for the first Assembly, members of a type displeasing to the governor. To retired officers of the British Army who were available, they preferred "one table men"—that is, men who drew no social line between their families and their hired help. Behind resistance to his purposes, open or disguised, the governor always detected disloyalty, democracy, and republicanism. When he was presented with a petition drafted by Rev. John Bethune, a Presbyterian minister, and largely signed, asking that the right of solemnizing marriage be extended to the ministers of all denominations, he denounced it as "the product of a wicked head and a most disloyal heart." Even in the guarded chamber of the Legislative Council, with its hand-picked membership, the horrid specter of republicanism raised its head; when two of its members disagreed with him on a matter of policy, he identified them as republicans. He asked forthwith for the appointment of a Captain Shaw "so that the plotters will have to face another staunch friend of the Constitution."

There was of course not a vestige of desire for the establishment of republican institutions on the part of those who thus failed to respond to the ardent young governor's enthusiasms; their resistance was nothing but the instinctive rallying of the mass of the people to the defence of modes, customs, habits of thought, social attitudes, and preference for simple democratic institutions in keeping with the North American tradition and with convictions which were part of their existence. Though they had fought and suffered for the royal cause they were not prepared willingly to accept a form of government which they knew to be not in keeping with their needs or their interests. Not that there was any organized formal resistance; the time for that had not yet come.

There were indeed influential residents who were enthusiastically in favor of the Simcoe policy of setting them apart from the generality of the people and conferring upon them power, privilege, and emoluments. These were the Loyalist gentry who had lost position, office, and wealth through their devotion to the cause of the King; and it was quite in keeping with the spirit in which the colonies of the Second Empire were being founded that they should be constituted the upper governing class in the new colony. Whatever his failures, Simcoe did succeed in imposing upon Upper Canada a nondemocratic form of government, in keeping with the blue prints, which in its strongholds of privilege and advantage held out for nearly half a century against a rising tide of opposition.

The Passing of the Old Order

This was the beginning of the long struggle between the conception, clearly envisaged from the outset and stoutly upheld, of the subordination of the colonies to the central imperial authority as the only possible basis for an empire; and the opposing principle of self-government which was carried, unconsciously, from the American colonies to the new settlement, there, growing slowly in darkness and obscurity, to become in the course of time the solvent, not only of the difficulties of Canada but of the problems of empire as well.

Not even in outline can the story of that long-extended struggle between opposing ideas of government be here told. Simcoe had not been ten years out of the country before the issue began to take form, and in another twenty years a majority of the members were demanding a transfer to the Assembly of the powers exercised by the close corporation made up of the governor and his nonrepresentative junta of advisers. Intrenched privilege fought all efforts at dislodgement by all the methods open to arbitrary power. By 1839 responsible government, which meant control of the executive by the elected body, was conceded in principle by Lord Durham in his famous report; and it was conceded, in fact and in practice, nine years later after a complete demonstration that the country could be governed on no other basis.

The critical and determining moment for Canada and for the whole Empire was that in which the issue of responsible government was settled: though the ultimate significance of the decision thus forced was far outside the ken of those who brought it about. They sought a solution for an intolerable local difficulty by a constitutional expedient which alone could bring relief; what, in fact, they did was to introduce an alien principle of government into the imperial system, which in the progress of the years undid the work of Pitt and Grenville and Dorchester and Simcoe and transformed the empire of privilege and central control into a brotherhood of democratic states.

The revolutionary character of the innovation was not hidden from those who resisted the change. What Governor Hutchinson said to the Legislature of Massachusetts in 1773 was said over and over again by the public men of Great Britain, by the resident governors to those who demanded the granting of responsible government. They posed the great constitutional dilemma to the advocates of change. How could the governor of a colony, an official of the British government subject to instructions from his superiors and responsible to them, also be obedient to the will of the people as expressed by a popular assembly? The thing, it was pointed out, simply could not be done. The ultimate authority had to be either the British government or the popular Assembly. If the latter, what would become of the Empire? Lord John Russell in his instructions to Poulett Thomson (afterwards Lord Sydenham), the first governor of Canada (created by the merger of Upper and Lower Canada in 1840), told him in effect that the case for responsible government was just so much nonsense. If the governor, Lord John explained, were to obey his instructions from the Queen (that is from Lord John and his colleagues of the British government) he could not accept conflicting advice from his executive council. If the conditions were such that he must accept the latter then "he is no longer a subordinate officer but an independent sovereign."[19] And of course by the same token the colony would become an independent nation. The logic could not be answered in terms; but it had to give way to the overriding logic of hard facts. It became evident that the colony had to be subjected to the autocratic rule of the governor, backed by force; or the people must govern themselves with the governor balancing himself as well as he could between two conflicting responsibilities—

[19] Russell to Thomson, Oct. 16, 1839, Kennedy's *Documents of the Canadian Constitution*, p. 423.

that to his elected advisers and that to the government overseas from which he derived his commission. Once this was made clear there was nothing for it but to concede self-government involving popular control of the executive.

If the British colonies had remained separate from one another and therefore small and impotent, the anomalies of the relationship created by this change might never have become apparent, and the "perfect subordination" in external matters which Durham stipulated might have continued. But other influences brought about first the union of the Canadas and later the federation of the colonies, thus creating the physical basis for a nation and making inevitable the emergence of conditions and situations which required the assertion and the exercise of powers inherent in nationhood.

Sixty years ago voices in Canada began to question the theory that the external affairs of Canada were the concern of the British government solely. Edward Blake, afterwards leader of the Liberal Party, in 1874 spoke of Canadians as "four million Britons who are not free" because they had no control over foreign policy. In 1882 David Mills, another Liberal leader, declared that if the rule that external relations must remain in the hands of the British government was unchangeable, it would be the destiny of the Empire to fall to pieces. No open effort was made to modify the theory but there was, as occasion arose, a polite usurpation of the powers, which, according to the original design of Empire, were the exclusive possession of the central authority, with a ready consent by the British government which showed that it recognized that the old order must pass away.

The situation was anomalous and potentially dangerous. That it could so long continue, giving rise to so little friction, is a high tribute to the capacity for practical adjustment and for putting realities above theories and dignities which inheres in British methods of government.

It needed only some international event of first importance affecting the Empire to make the anomaly no longer tolerable; and this the War supplied. The declaration of the relationship among the British nations, necessitated by the development of events, which was made at the meeting of the Imperial Conference in 1917, in war time, was a reaffirmation of the principle put forward unavailingly by the leaders of the American colonists on the eve of the Revolution.[20] This theory of empire relations, accepted as a basis of adjustment by the British in 1917, was redefined in terms wider and more exact at the Imperial Con-

[20] The text of the constitutional declaration adopted by the Imperial War Cabinet, 1917, at the instance of Sir Robert Borden, Prime Minister of Canada, will be found in Kennedy's *Documents of the Canadian Constitution*, p. 698. It declared that the impending readjustment of the constitutional relations of the component parts of the Empire "should be based upon a full recognition of the Dominions as autonomous nations of an Imperial Commonwealth." See also Zimmern, *The Third British Empire*, p. 28.

ference of 1926, and given formal legal sanctions in the Westminster Statute of 1931.

Thus the Second Empire passed; and the British Commonwealth of Nations came into being, firmly based upon the foundation stone of principle which had been rejected in favor of an appeal to the sword just 150 years earlier. The wisdom of the potential rebels of 1774 and 1775 was thus vindicated; but a little too late to save all North America to the Empire. But if North America by reasons of the mistakes of long ago is now and must remain divided politically, it is nevertheless in a larger sense a unity. It remains a stronghold of democracy, a citadel of the English-speaking world.

II
CANADA AS A DEMOCRACY

II

CANADA AS A DEMOCRACY

The Coming of Responsible Government

I HAVE already sketched, in the merest outline, the growth, development and final emergence of Canada as a democratic nation. Some of the gaps in the earlier sketch I now propose to fill in, because this is necessary if we are to come to an intelligent estimate of the part which American influences played in the making of Canada.

After the loss of the thirteen colonies a vast stretch of the North American continent remained British, but this wilderness was broken by only two struggling colonies: Quebec, newly taken from the French, alien in language and religion; and Nova Scotia. From those inauspicious beginnings there has grown the Dominion of Canada of today, a country which, though far outdistanced in population, wealth and strength by its vast neighbor, is nevertheless not negligible among the nations of the earth. For the making of this nation there had to be a steady extension of its physical basis and the progressive development of its institutions of government. In the founding of the various colonial settlements which in due time came together to form the Dominion of Canada there was no thought of nationhood or of democracy; they were intended to be and to remain provinces subordinate to the rule of Great Britain. It was fifty years before they attained a working measure of self-government; and it was not until after this stage was reached that the processes of consolidation and expansion began. It took another sixty years for the Federation to emerge and develop to its present appearance of finality; and it was only yesterday that its constitutional development came to its full flowering.

To this long development of growth, change, and adjustment, external influences from the neighboring republic contributed; the country was in special degree open to them because, with the exception of Quebec, it lacked such defensive and repelling powers as differences of religion, of language and institutions. I have already tried to indicate the extent and value of the endowment in political instinct and belief which the foundation populations of the English Canadian colonies took with them from their earlier environment. This was derived, not from the new Republic, but from a political society antecedent to it; but the impact of the Republic and its people upon the newer British communities continued, and has been during the whole period of our existence, and is to this day in almost every aspect of our national life, a factor of high importance. Before I deal with the institutions and the governmental system which are the working agencies of the Canadian democracy, it will not, I think, be out of place briefly to consider some of the

American influences which were inescapable in view of the circumstances.

For the earlier years I limit my inquiry to Upper Canada, where the interlacement of interests was greatest. I have referred to the Loyalist immigrants as constituting the foundation population of Upper Canada. This population was soon overlaid by a second and a larger influx from the United States. Governor Simcoe abounded in strongly-held convictions; one was that a large proportion of the people of the United States were yearning to resume their British citizenship. He therefore let it be known, through the border settlements, that those who held these sentiments would be welcome to Upper Canada, where there was free land for the asking. The trusting governor assumed that the activating motive, when an immigrant made his appearance, was rather a desire to renew allegiance than to obtain land. The Duke de la Rochefoucauld, who visited Governor Simcoe, records in his account of his travels a conversation between the governor and an immigrant whom he met by chance on the forest trail.

You are tired [said Simcoe] of the federal government; you like not any longer to have so many kings; you wish for your old father. You are perfectly right. Come along, we love such good Royalists as you are: we will give you land.[1]

[1] *John Graves Simcoe,* by D. C. Scott, "Makers of Canada Series," Toronto, 1910, pp. 56 ff.

The immigration thus induced continued in increasing volume until, by the time it was stopped by the war of 1812, about half the residents of Upper Canada were Americans who had come into the country during the preceding eighteen years, many, perhaps most, of whom were of Revolutionary stock. Only a small proportion of these settlers, however, showed sympathy with the invaders in the War of 1812 and found it necessary, when the attempted conquest failed, to leave the country. Nevertheless those who remained fell under the suspicion of the government. Efforts were made to deprive them of a citizenship which previously had been assumed to have been bestowed with the grant of land, and to harass them in various ways. This was due perhaps less to their American birth than to the fact that, in the political alignment then taking place, they allied themselves solidly with the reform elements which were demanding an extension of popular government. This question of the status of American-born residents was in issue for nearly twenty years until a Reform majority in the Assembly forced a satisfactory settlement.

The twenty years before the so-called rebellion of 1837 constituted a highly critical period in Canadian history which still awaits adequate treatment by historians. It is customary to deal with it as though the issues between the conflicting parties, which were fought over during this period, were plain to see and easy to understand, whereas they were in fact somewhat complex. The factor, which still awaits critical examination and appraisement, is the extent, character and purpose of the contribution to the political struggle made by the powerful American elements in the Reform Party of Upper Canada.

There is no mystery about what the government party believed in and fought for. The control of the province was in the hands of a highly efficient and thoroughly organized upper class which filled all the offices, dominated the professions, distributed the public revenues in ways most pleasing and profitable to themselves, practised nepotism unblushingly, and held all the reins of government. Each governor in turn was absorbed into this organization. He was indispensable to it because he threw over its programs and performances the prestige of the crown. But it was not a mere governing clique; it had a popular following which enabled it to win alternate elections. A Reform control of the Assembly with its protestations, inquiries and memorials, almost invariably led to a Tory rally with victory at the next election. And the cry by which victory was won, with the governor often sounding the note, was that the reformers desired to bring in American systems of administration and government, looking to separation from Great Britain, and ultimate union with the United States. The stock observation upon this charge has been to denounce it as a libel on the reformers who, it is declared, sought only to regularize government methods by bringing them into conformity with the British practice. That this was indeed the purpose of that substantial wing of the Reform Party which accepted the Baldwins, father and son, as leaders is undoubted; but research work in the political literature of the time certainly tends to give some measure of support to the Tory charges, at least to this extent, that many of the changes and reforms urged by elements in the Reform party were obviously suggested by the experience of the United States. This was especially the case when the formulation of policy was in the hands of Marshall Spring Bidwell, a native of Massachusetts. He led the party in the disastrous election campaign of 1836, when Sir Francis Bond Head, the new governor, took the stump on behalf of the Tories.[2] Exasperation over their defeat resulted in the extreme elements of the party, under the leadership of William Lyon Mackenzie, a perfervid Scot, raising the standard of rebellion and declaring for a republic. This so compromised Bidwell, though historians acquit him of complicity, that he obeyed the order of the governor to leave the country. He thereupon removed to the state of New York, where he had a career as a lawyer of some distinction.

[2] "He [Sir Francis Bond Head, the governor] sincerely believed he was fighting for British connexion and British institutions and perhaps he was. The programme with which the Reformers confronted him —elective Legislative Council, control of all revenues by the Assembly, the British Government to keep its hands completely off colonial legislation—was an American programme." Chester New, *Lord Durham, A Biography of John George Lambton, First Earl of Durham,* Oxford, The Clarendon Press, 1929, p. 343.

These events were naturally regarded by the victorious party as amply justifying their estimates of the Reform program and the ends it had in view. When, subsequently, in consequence of the effect upon English public opinion of the uprisings and their suppression with drastic punishments of exile and death, they found it necessary to give an account of the reasons for the outbreak, the American residents in Upper Canada were cast in responsible rôles. A Committee of the Legislative Council by an official report gave themselves, in their capacity as members of the ruling combination, a testimonial of complete innocence; in their identification of the guilty parties they had this to say:

Your Committee are of opinion that the proximity of the American frontier—the wild and chimerical notions of civil government broached and discussed there—the introduction of a very great number of border Americans into this province as settlers who, with some most respectable and worthy exceptions, formed the bulk of the reformers, who carried their opinions so far as disaffection . . . emboldened a portion of the minority to rise in rebellion in the hope of achieving the overthrow of the government with foreign assistance. Is it [the report went on to ask] because reformers or a portion of them can command the sympathies of the United States and of Lower Canadian rebels that the internal affairs of a British Colony must be conducted to please them?[3]

On the morrow of their triumph, which as they

[3] Kennedy, *Documents of the Canadian Constitution,* pp. 374 ff.

doubtless thought permanently insured their position, the Tories met with humiliation and overthrow. Though the rebellion in Upper Canada hardly exceeded a riot in dimensions, it outweighed in political effectiveness the much more serious uprising of the French Canadians in Lower Canada, because it was an indication of the alienation of a formidable political party in an English-speaking province from the scheme of government which Great Britain had established and was delighted to uphold. The affair was altogether too reminiscent of the American Revolution. Lord Durham was dispatched posthaste to Canada in the capacity of High Commissioner; and at the same time Robert Baldwin rose to a position of undisputed leadership in the Reform Party. It did not require the recent discovery in the Durham papers of a memorandum from Baldwin to Durham[4] in which the doctrine of responsible government is set forth in detail, to make it evident that there was a measure of understanding and agreement between Durham and those reformers who sought a solution for the problem in the application to Canada of the British system of responsible government and parliamentary control. In the report of the Committee of the Legislative Council, already referred to, in which the exasperation of the doomed oligarchy finds acrid expression, Lord Durham is accused of taking his in-

[4] *Report of Canadian Archives, 1928.* The text is given in Kennedy, *op. cit.,* p. 335.

formation about Upper Canada from some person unnamed in the report "who has evidently entered on his task, with the desire to exalt the opponents of the Colonial government in the estimation of the High Commissioner and to throw discredit on the statements of the supporters of British influence, and British connections."

Lord Durham, in his great report, and in the dispatches which preceded it, took a line which was maddening to the oligarchy. In place of falling in with its idea that the way to combat American influence was to discourage intercourse and to keep, by arbitrary rule, a firm control over the population, he saw the situation of Canada, existing and in the future, in the light of its relations to the United States. He saw that the conditions of living in the British colonies, as controlled by such factors as municipal institutions, provision for education, participation by the people in the government, contrasted most unfavorably with those in the adjoining states; and he knew that the perpetuation of these conditions would strengthen the desire, already sporadically present in the colonies, for absorption by the United States. Attempts to check this by the application of force based upon the power of Great Britain would strengthen the interventionist mood of the American people, already somewhat in evidence.

There are two pregnant passages to this effect in the report:

If by such means the British nation shall be content to retain a barren and injurious sovereignty, it will but tempt the chances of foreign aggression by keeping continually exposed to a powerful and ambitious neighbor a distant dependency, in which an invader would find no resistance but might rather reckon on active coöperation from a portion of the resident population. . . .[5]

The maintenance of an absolute form of government on any part of the North American continent can never continue for any long time without exciting a general feeling in the United States against a power of which the existence is secured by means so odious to the people.[6]

The side note to the paragraph in which this significant statement is made reads: "Importance of preserving the sympathy of the United States."

The purposes of Lord Durham were to meet the demand for self-government by concessions, based upon British practice and precedent, which would be in themselves so satisfactory and so capable of development that the disgruntled element would accept them in lieu of possible American expedients to which it had been giving consideration; and further to check the tendency to look to union with the United States as the only road to the deeper satisfaction of citizenship by giving it the vision of nationhood. "If we wish," he wrote, "to prevent the extension of this [American] influence it can only be done by raising

[5] *Lord Durham's Report on the Affairs of British North America*, ed. by Sir C. P. Lucas, Oxford, The Clarendon Press, 1912, II, 264.
[6] *Idem*, II, 297.

up for the North American colonist some nationality of his own; by elevating these small and unimportant communities into a society having some objects of a national importance; and by thus giving their inhabitants a country which they will be unwilling to see absorbed even into one more powerful."[7] In these parts of his report Durham as in a vision foresaw the future nation and its essential foundation: self-government on British lines; the union of the North American colonies; and the development of the spirit of nationality. Time and the labors of others turned the vision into reality; and his estimate of the consequences of these changes has been justified in the widest measure by actual results. They removed from Canada that desire for the adoption of American institutions which, if acted upon, would have been the forerunner of political union. This general statement is not affected by the episode of the Montreal manifesto of 1849, calling for annexation, which was an expression of temporary pique by the most British element of the population, enraged by their ejection from power, and the simultaneous loss of their preferential markets in Great Britain.

From this time forth there was universal acceptance by Canadians of the British parliamentary system as the most effective agency of democratic government. Confederation came thirty years later, supplying the physical basis of a nation; and in this area the rising

[7] *Idem*, II, 311.

spirit of nationality, employing the machinery of self-government, built the Canada of today, which divides the North American continent with the United States and exemplifies north of the line the British principles of democratic government in contrast with those which are known to the world as American.

But I have been very inadequate in setting out the antecedent causes of this great and beneficent development if I have not made clear to you that the direct and indirect effects of the impact of the United States upon the colonies bulks high among these causes.

The Influences That Made Confederation

The second great contribution by the United States to the making of the Canadian nation had to do with the creation of the Canadian Federation. It would not be correct to say that the inspiration for federal union came from the desire of the colonies to follow the example of the United States; but it can be said that confederation could not have been brought about at the time it was affected had it not been for conditions which were the Canadian reaction to American events. One might also say that if confederation had not been brought about at that time, it might have been found impossible later to accomplish it. In quieter times, with political feelings less in control of human wills, the economic resistance to a union of the colonies might have proved all-powerful. We have a conventional account of the making of confederation which takes little note of the forces that operated behind the façade, which misplaces the sequences of cause and effect, and misjudges the significance of events.

From the beginning of the second Empire there had been, at intervals, suggestions of a union of the British colonies in North America under a common direction; but confederation was not the culmination of leisurely academic discussion. The project, which was launched in 1858 and proceeded rapidly to completion, had its origins in the realities and necessities of the times. One of its roots was the attitude of indifference or fatalism taken toward the Canadian colonies in the decade following the conceding of responsible government by leading British public men. They accepted the view that in striving for self-government the people of the colonies were taking the first steps toward an inevitable separation; this found expression, sometimes in official documents, in the highest quarters.[8] Disraeli thinks that these wretched colonies, soon to be independent, are in the meantime "millstones around our neck." Earl Grey can see no British interest served by retaining them. Lord John Russell, speaking as Prime Minister in the House of Commons, looks forward philosophically to their independence. This feeling continued through-

[8] For an accurate, condensed account of the attitude of British political leaders toward the British North American colonies, see "British Opinion and Canadian Autonomy," in *British Supremacy & Canadian Self-Government, 1839-1854*, by J. L. Morison, Glasgow, 1919.

out the fifties: and was strengthened by the realization, following the outbreak of the American Civil War, that the North American colonies were dangerous liabilities—they were referred to by the permanent head of the Colonial Office "as a sort of damnosa hereditas." Tennyson lashed out in anger at this mood:

> And that true north of which we lately heard
> A strain to shame us, loose the bonds and go.

My own reading of those times is that the movement for confederation, which began in the province of Canada in the late fifties, was the reply of leading colonials to this British attitude, of which they were aware, and which they resented. The colonies, divided and weak, did not want independence. The people knew that to independence there was an inevitable sequel: absorption by the United States. There may have been a desire in the thirties of the nineteenth century for annexation to the United States, but with the granting of self-government it vanished. The Canadian public man who first realized the situation was Alexander Galt, a son of John Galt, the Scotch novelist; and he set himself resolutely to deal with it. He is the real father of confederation. Reading and collating his speeches from his first advocacy of the project to his post-confederation comments upon it, one can see what was in his mind. If the colonies were united they would have some chance of surviving even if they were told to "loose the bonds and go"; perhaps as a confederation Great Britain would be glad to retain them as a coördinate or subordinate nation. In 1858 he journeyed to England to acquaint the government with his plans and enlist its sympathy. His representations to Bulwer Lytton, Secretary for the Colonies, that as things were shaping in British North America, there must be a choice between the confederation of the provinces and their absorption by the United States, left that gentleman and his colleagues quite unimpressed. Returning from England empty-handed, he was unable further to interest his colleagues in the project.

But events were moving. D'Arcy McGee, newly arrived in Canada from Ireland, via the United States, where he sojourned some years, allied himself with Galt; and as his occupation was that of a lecturer, he familiarized audiences in all the British provinces with the idea that it was necessary for their existence that the colonies should come together. The outbreak of the Civil War in the United States, followed by difficulties between the governments of the United States and Great Britain, made the colonists conscious of the dangers of their position. It suggested possibilities to which they had to give attention—the possibility of war between the United States and Great Britain; the possibility of the northern states, in the event of losing the South, finding compensation in overrunning the colonies, which they could easily do with their

mighty armies.[9] The southern confederacy had open
and powerful sympathizers in Canada, some of them
highly placed; the relations between the British countries and the United States were in a dangerously
strained condition; the newspapers of the northern
states were filled with threats, to be carried out in the
future, against Canada.[10] To understand the situation,
it is necessary only to read the speeches by public
men, in which confederation was recommended to the
people. McGee in a public address warned Canadians
of their danger:

That shot fired at Fort Sumter was the signal gun of
a new epoch for North America which told the people
of Canada, more plainly than human speech can ever express it, to sleep no more, except on their arms—unless
in their sleep they desire to be overtaken and subjugated.
. . . I do not believe that it is our destiny to be engulfed
into a Republican union, renovated and inflamed with

[9] This apprehension was felt in the highest quarters. Queen Vic-
toria in her diaries, under date of Feb. 12, 1865, writes of a conversation which she had with a cabinet minister about "America
and the danger, which seems approaching of our having a war with
her, as soon as she makes peace; of the impossibility of our being able
to hold Canada but we must struggle for it; and far the best would
be to let it go as an independent kingdom under an English prince."
[10] The advisability of Canada assuming independence as a protection
against American imperialism was urged by Goldwin Smith in a
letter to the *London Daily News*, Jan. 1862, occasioned by the Trent
incident. "There is," he wrote, "but one way to make Canada im-
pregnable and that is to fence her round with the majesty of an
independent nation. To invade and conquer an independent nation,
without provocation, is an act from which in the present state of
opinion, even the Americans would recoil." *The Empire: A series of
letters published in the Daily News, 1862, 1863* by Goldwin Smith.
Oxford & London: John Henry & James Parker, 1863.

the wine of victory, of which she now drinks so deeply—
it seems to me that we have theatre enough under our
feet to act another and a worthier part; we can hardly
join the Americans on our own terms, and we never
ought to join them on theirs.[11]

"Events stronger than advocacy, stronger than man,
have come in at last," said McGee, speaking in the
Canadian Parliament in support of confederation.[12]
It was in this speech that McGee spoke of the three
warnings that Canada had been given: The warning
from England that Canada must look after her own
defense; the warning from the United States—the notice to abrogate the reciprocity treaty, the threat to
arm the lakes, the enormous expansion of the American Army and Navy; the breakdown of parliamentary
government in the colony. If this be discounted as
the rhodomontade of a professional orator, we can
turn to the speech of George Brown, in the same de-
bate, for a still apter quotation: "The civil war in the
neighboring republic; the possibility of war between
Great Britain and the United States; the threatened
repeal of the reciprocity treaty; the threatened aboli-
tion of the American bonding system; the unsettled
position of the Hudson's Bay company, and the

[11] Thomas D'Arcy McGee, *Speeches and Addresses Chiefly on the Subject of British American Union,* London, 1865, pp. 34-35.
[12] *Parliamentary Debates on the Subject of the Confederation of the
British North American Provinces,* 3d Session, 8th Provincial Parliament of Canada, Quebec, 1865, 1032 pp., pp. 132 ff. Hereafter
referred to as *Confederation Debates.* Also Skelton, Isabel (Murphy),
Thomas D'Arcy McGee, Quebec, 1925; Toronto, 1930, pp. 496 ff.

changed feeling of England as to the relations of great colonies to the parent state; all combine at this moment to arrest earnest attention to the gravity of the situation and unite us all in one vigorous effort to meet the emergency like men."[13]

These reasons for union by the provinces were as potent in Great Britain as in Canada, for though official and political opinion there still tended to the acceptance of the belief that the colonies would ultimately become independent, there was deep apprehension over the possibility that they might be absorbed forcibly by the American republic. Speaking in the Commons in 1862 the Secretary of State for War, Sir George Cornewall Lewis, expressed this opinion quite bluntly: "I for one can only say that I look forward without apprehension, and I may add, without regret, to the time when Canada might become an independent state, [hear, hear,] but I think it behooves England not to cast Canada loose or send her adrift before she has acquired sufficient strength to assert her own independence."

To avert this fate of absorption by the United States, believed to be impending, the British government began to back the movement for confederation with all the influence it could command. That the scheme did not crash because of opposition in the

[13] George Brown, the leader of the Liberal Party who joined forces with his political and personal enemy, John A. Macdonald, to make Confederation possible. The quotation is from *Confederation Debates*, p. 114.

Maritimes was plainly due to the open and somewhat unblushing intervention of British authority. With all difficulties surmounted, the Dominion of Canada came into being July 1, 1867.

The Dominion of Canada thus constituted included only the provinces between Lake Superior and the Atlantic Ocean; but within four years its area was multiplied seven times by the transfer to it by the British government of its North American territories, and the inclusion in the federation of the province of British Columbia. Again the reason for this rapid and, in an economic sense, rash expansion was political; and again the impulse to political action came from the United States. In the years following the Civil War "manifest destiny" was a bright alluring star to many American statesmen.[14] In Washington Senators Sumner and Chandler and Hamilton Fish, Secretary of State, were fascinated with the prospect of taking over Canada in part payment of the bill against Great Britain, on the score of the "Alabama" and other activities, which Senator Sumner worked out at two and a half billion dollars—a proposition upon which the British minister was actually sounded. Americans of the northwestern states thought the hour had struck for taking into the Union the vast wilderness of Rupert's Land. A Minnesota senator proposed in the Senate a resolution favoring a treaty which would

[14] Keenleyside, H. L., *Canada and the United States: Some Aspects of the History of the Republic and the Dominion*, New York, 1929, pp. 139, 160, 161, 165, 302.

transfer to the American Union all British territory west of 90 degrees' longitude. In the isolated, helpless pioneer province of British Columbia, far out on the Pacific Coast, there was an open and active agitation for union with the United States, drawing support and encouragement from the other side of the boundary. The purchase of Alaska meant to Seward that the whole Pacific coast was to become part of the United States.[15]

With these warning signals flying, the Canadian government and the British government in coöperation moved swiftly to checkmate the plans of the Washington expansionists. The northwestern territory and Rupert's Land within three years were added to Canada, carrying the Dominion's boundaries west to the Rocky Mountains and north to the Pole. British Columbia, with a legislature to deal with in which the policy of annexation commanded strong support, was a more difficult problem; but steady pressure from the British government and a pledge, impossible of fulfillment, from Canada that within ten years a transcontinental railway would be built, finally proved effective; and in 1871 the motto of Canada "from sea to sea" was made good. Thus within thirteen years, from the launching by Galt of his drive for federal

[15] To Senator Sumner the acquisition of Alaska had a still wider significance. Speaking in the United States Senate April 7, 1867, he said: "The present treaty is a visible step in the occupation of the whole American continent. As such it will be recognized by the world and accepted by the American people."

union, the whole of British North America, with the exception of two islands (one of which came in two years later) was brought under a common national authority. The pressure that drove the statesmen forward in a race, as they believed against time, was the fear, real or imagined, that unless they succeeded in their plans the American dream of "manifest destiny" would be achieved.

The Winning of Legislative Independence

The new Dominion of Canada, though it spanned a continent, remained a colony; this was made most clear by the British North America Act which brought it into being. Its self-governing powers were limited to domestic questions; and even in these spheres it was subject to an overriding authority when the British Parliament passed laws imperial in their scope and intention. The governor-general was also an imperial official with special responsibilities. The right of the King to disallow Canadian legislation, upon the advice of his British ministers, was affirmed. The external relations of the Dominion were wholly in the hands of the British Foreign Office. Thus the Dominion of Canada began its existence in 1867 with a system of government substantially in keeping with the terms of the compromise which had been submitted to the British government by the first American Congress ninety-three years before, and had been rejected by it. The "perfect subordination" of the colony to the metropolis in all matters of external policy stipulated by Durham still continued and had the appearance of permanency.

The inadequacy of the system by which Great Britain looked after their external affairs was recognized at once by the Canadians when they came to have dealings with the United States. Their instinctive feeling was that their interests would be better served if they attended to the job themselves. Even before confederation the British American colonies sent unofficial representatives to Washington in an attempt to save the reciprocity treaty, to the great scandal of Lord Lyons, the British Ambassador, who in vigorous letters to the Governor-General of Canada and the Foreign Minister of Great Britain, protested this irruption of amateurs into his preserve. The movement by which Canada won the right to control her foreign affairs was in the established tradition. It began deferentially, pursued its purpose over a long period of years, established precedents from which new advances could be made, and attained its end at last by an aggressive stroke. In 1870 the propriety of Canada seeking power directly to negotiate commercial treaties was urged unavailingly in the Canadian Parliament by Galt. Recognizing Canadian feeling on this question, the British government in 1871 appointed Sir John A. Macdonald, the Canadian Prime Minister, one of the six British plenipotentiaries who negotiated the Treaty of Washington. His experience with his

British colleagues—knowledge of which became general in Canada—strengthened the Canadians in their belief that they had better look after their own affairs in treaty making, in fact if not in form. "My colleagues," Sir John A. Macdonald wrote, "were continually pressing me to yield; I was obliged to stand out and, I am afraid, to make myself extremely disagreeable to them."

The lesson of this was not lost and three years later when negotiations were renewed looking to the settlement of questions outstanding between the United States and Canada, the Canadian government insisted that the British plenipotentiaries should be only two in number: George Brown of Canada and the British Minister at Washington. The treaty was completed and signed. It provided, among other things, for the renewal of the former reciprocity treaty; for reciprocity in coasting; for a joint commission to look after boundary waters; and for the enlargement of the Canadian canals, including those on the St. Lawrence. This enlightened treaty was evidence of vast improvement in the relations between at least the governments of the two countries. Had it been in effect for the twenty-one-year period, for which it was negotiated, it would have profoundly affected for all time the relations between the two countries. Do you ask what became of this treaty? It has its place of rest in what John Hay called the "grave-yard of treaties"—the United States Senate.

The precedent of 1874 was thereafter followed in all treaty negotiations in which Canadian interests were predominant. Negotiations were in the hands of the British plenipotentiary who was appointed at the instance of the Canadian government. The resulting treaty or convention represented the view of the Canadian government; but the ratification rested with the British government. This procedure, however, did not quiet the agitation in Canada for the right of direct negotiation. In 1882 and again in 1892 the Liberal opposition raised the issue in Parliament, contending that the proximity of Canada to the United States and the intimacy of their relationships made it necessary that they should be able to deal with one another directly. When they attained office the Liberals did not press this claim but in practice they kept the making of commercial treaties in their own hands, the purely British contribution being nominal. In the negotiations which led up to the reciprocity agreement of 1911 the part played by the British Minister at Washington was that of simply introducing the Canadian Ministers to the American Secretary of State.

Twelve years later a Liberal government in Canada seized the occasion, offered by negotiations with the government of the United States, to claim—and give practical effect to the claim—that Canada was in control of her external relations. The antecedent circumstances suggested that the time was ripe for this final step. In 1917 there had been the declaration by the

Imperial Conference that the relationship among the British nations was one of equality. Canada's representatives at the Peace Conference attended under powers given by the King upon the advice of his Canadian ministers. Canada, as a member of the League of Nations, was subordinate to no other member nation. Canada's status of nationhood and her equality with Great Britain had been affirmed by leading public men in Canada and in Great Britain alike. The Canadian government, having meditated upon these developments, decided, when the need of an arrangement with the United States for the protection of the halibut fisheries of the north Pacific became pressing, to put this claim of nationhood to the test by undertaking to make the treaty one between the Dominion of Canada, a nation of North America, and the United States, another North American nation. The Canadian government appointed Mr. Lapointe, Minister of Justice, plenipotentiary, securing powers for him from the King; Mr. Lapointe negotiated the treaty, and signed it alone as the representative of Canada and not as the representative of the British Empire as previously had been invariably the case.

The significance of this act was not realized until the deed was done; there then arose a tremendous clamor in Canada, in Great Britain, and in all parts of the British Empire. In strict law Canada was in 1923 a dependent country wholly incapable of completing an international instrument. What the Canadian government did was calmly to assume that the constitutional right to equality and nationhood, which had been recognized, carried with it, of necessity, the legal power to make these rights effective. This daring innovation, entirely at variance with the traditional British way of having legal rights slowly overlaid and destroyed by successive deposits of precedents representing the growth of constitutional rights, brought definitely to a close the experiment in imperialism upon which Great Britain embarked on the morrow of the American Revolution. One of the formerly dependent colonies had in fact established its independence of control by the British government and the British Parliament, and thereby revealed the fact that the Second Empire had made way for the Commonwealth. The situation created by Canada in 1923 had to be accepted and regularized; and there followed in inevitable succession the recognition by the Conference of 1923 of the right of the Dominion to make treaties, the Balfour declaration of 1926, the meeting of the constitutional committee in 1929, and the passing of the Westminster Act in 1931.

To the chain of events, with the results which I have indicated, no conscious contribution was made by the United States nor by any agency American in character. I have already said the United States pursued its own interests and applied the policies which it regarded as appropriate; the conditions thus created, as they affected Canada, led to adjustments which affected, one way or another, national movements. These Canadian developments toward parliamentary independence and nationhood were displeasing to many Canadians; they hoped for a federal union of the British nations instead. In expressing their regrets at what has come to pass they are somewhat inclined to hold the United States in large measure responsible for what happened. But those Canadians who promoted this movement toward nationhood and were always conscious of the objectives they sought will give the American government and their people a clean bill of health in this regard. They undoubtedly contributed, but this was done by inadvertence.

Let me illustrate this by a brief reference to an American-Canadian episode, long forgotten, I imagine, by Americans, which, in my judgment, is one of the prime reasons why Canada today is in complete charge of her external affairs. My reference is to the Alaskan boundary controversy, which was settled by the finding of the Alaska Commission in 1903.[16] A majority made up of the three United States commissioners and Lord Alverstone, the nominee of the British government, made the award; the two Canadian commissioners refused to sign it on the ground that the finding was political, not judicial, and that it ignored the just rights of Canada. The details of

[16] There is a full discussion of the Alaskan boundary controversy from the Canadian standpoint in J. W. Dafoe's *Clifford Sifton in Relation to His Times,* Toronto, 1931, Chap. VIII.

this controversy cannot be here stated even in outline; it is necessary for the present argument only to say that from the circumstances antecedent to the meeting of the Commission and from the proceedings of the Commission itself, the people of Canada came to suspect that the Commission was a political, not a judicial body, which would, under diplomatic pressure from Washington, reject the Canadian case. The confirmation, to the Canadian mind, of these suspicions by the course taken by the Canadian commissioners was followed by an outburst of popular wrath, surprising in its depth and intensity. Instinctively, the sure safeguard against future mishaps of this kind occurred to great numbers of Canadians, and expression was given to their feelings by Canadian public men who had an intimate knowledge of the circumstances which attended the hearing of the dispute. "The difficulty as I conceive it to be," said Sir Wilfrid Laurier, Prime Minister, in Parliament, "is that so long as Canada remains a dependency of the British Crown, the present powers that we have are not sufficient for the maintenance of our rights." He foretold a demand upon the British Parliament for additional rights "so that if we ever have to deal with matters of a similar nature again, we shall deal with them in our own way, in our own fashion, according to the best light we have." Mr. A. B. Aylesworth, one of the Canadian commissioners, in a newspaper interview expressed the same view. Clifford Sifton, a member of the Canadian government, who had had charge of the Canadian case, was outspoken. In the future, he said, in similar cases, all the commissioners should be Canadians; "a somewhat radical readjustment will have to be made before a great while."

It is my belief that the movement for enlarging Canada's powers to those of nationhood took definite form at that time. Perhaps on this point I might repeat what I have already said in my biography of Clifford Sifton:

In this strong illumination of the inadequacies of the existing relationship and with the revelation to themselves of their national spirit, the Canadian people passed at a single stride from the plane of willing dependency to one of conscious aspiration for the powers of nationhood. A definite turning was taken, although the goal lay far down the years.

So little did the United States authorities know about the constitutional developments that were going on in Canada that the enterprise upon which Canada embarked in 1923 in entering into direct diplomatic relations with the United States nearly suffered shipwreck at their hands. The draft of the halibut treaty made by the United States Department of State made the British Empire as a whole the other party to the arrangement. When this difficulty was straightened out and the completed treaty was submitted to the Senate, that august body added a reservation that made it, in effect, an empire treaty. Incidentally, by the wording of the reservation, it was revealed that the Senate thought that Canada was a part of Great Britain. This setback to their plans did not seriously embarrass the Canadian government. The Canadian Parliament ratified the original treaty and awaited with dignity and patience the withdrawal by the United States of its reservation. This was done quietly and discreetly the following year. Perhaps this was the first time an outside nation brought the United States Senate to time; if, so, it was a considerable achievement for Canada in the first exercise of her claimed powers.

With the acceptance, by all parties, of the principle that each British nation could, at will, take charge of its foreign affairs, Canada proceeded to establish a number of legations. It was inevitable that Washington should be chosen as the home of the first of these legations, since it was the variety, complexity and importance of our relations with the United States that led to recognition by Canada of the necessity of taking charge of her own affairs abroad. We have sent distinguished Canadians to Washington and have had the honor of receiving worthy representatives of the President of the United States. That these two nations should have intimate and direct diplomatic relations is so reasonable, so in keeping with commonsense, that the arrangement takes on the appearance of being part of the natural order of things; and there is difficulty in remembering that less than ten years ago this was a subject of bitter controversy in Canada.

Canada an Actual Democracy

The recorded facts are, I think, conclusive that it was the essential North Americanism of the Canadian people that led them into courses of thought and action with which the theory of government embodied in the Second Empire could not be permanently reconciled. If Canada had been an island a thousand miles removed from the American coast the constitutional development of Canada would have been, in all likelihood, along very different lines; the federation of the British nations with a common government might have been attainable. Canada must take the responsibility in history of having first made unworkable the original plan of empire government: a central authority that commanded and colonies that obeyed; and of then making impossible the solution which would have been preferable to Great Britain and to the Australasian Dominions. The present British Commonwealth of Nations resulted from the adoption of successive expedients for the purpose of keeping Canada in the family; this is the plain fact, simply stated.

What those in Canada who resisted the movement, and those in the other British nations who deplored it, could never understand, was that in this there was no attempt to imitate the institutions and political customs of the United States, and certainly no intention of furthering a merger of the two countries. They could not realize that this was an indigenous development, looking to the building up on the North American continent of a nation which would be free to develop in its own way, and also to borrow and adapt methods and institutions from kindred nations near at hand or overseas, provided that this put no impediment in the way of the development of national sentiment. They should have been satisfied that there was no intention that the new nation should play the "sedulous ape" to the United States by the fact that there was everywhere in Canada an acceptance of the British methods of government as the readiest, the most adjustable and the most effective means of equipping a democracy to govern itself. In the organization of our parties, in the methods by which political campaigns are waged, in superficial aspects of our federal system, there are resemblances between Canada and the United States; but in the thing that really matters, the means by which the Canadian democracy makes the policies of the country and determines its courses, we have adapted to our own ends the British methods of government which have developed down the centuries. In our adaptation of these methods to the service of democracy we, with Australia, set the pace for Great Britain. In the home land of representative and responsible government it was long held that this system was workable only if the body of political power, which made governments and to which they were answerable, was aristocratic with a mere infusion of democracy. But in the British colonies there was not the offset of an organized aristocratic society and, once responsible government was conceded, democracies of these colonies had put into their hands the most direct and effective system of popular government yet devised—to the great alarm of the governing society of Great Britain, as I have already shown by appropriate quotations. In the extension of the franchise, to the ultimate granting of adult suffrage, the Dominions were decades in advance of Great Britain.

Lord Bryce, in his *Modern Democracies,* saluted Canada as "an actual democracy." In Canada, he said, "better perhaps than in any other country, the working of the English system can be judged in its application to the facts of a new and swiftly growing country, thoroughly democratic in its ideas and its institutions."[17] This system of government developed in a unitary state; and many of the misconceptions about Canada, as well as most of our internal troubles arise from the fact that these had to be adapted to a federation. The Dominion of Canada could only come into being as a federal state, as Sir John A. Macdonald admitted when he reluctantly gave up his hope of a legislative union. We speak of the Constitution of Canada but we have no instrument of government comparable to that of the United States. If Canada were a unitary state we should no more have a written constitution than Great Britain has. There is no constitutional limitation upon the legislative power in Great Britain or in Canada. But in Canada the legislative powers

[17] Bryce, James, *Modern Democracies,* New York, 1921, I, 455.

have been divided between the Dominion and the
provinces in proportions which it apparently defies
the wit of man and the learning of judges to define.
After sixty years of judicial interpretation the confusion is greater than at the beginning. This arises in
part from the fact that the last word on our Constitution is said by a court—the Judicial Committee of the
Privy Council—which has no native understanding of
a federal system. This was very strikingly shown many
years ago when no less a person than the Lord Chancellor, hearing argument in an appeal from Australia,
expressed his puzzlement at the claim that the law,
which was the occasion for the lawsuit, was unconstitutional. His Lordship could not really understand
how an Act of Parliament could be unconstitutional.[18]
When the constitutionality of an act is challenged in
Canada, the action means nothing more than the
charge that the act has been passed by the province
when the power is actually vested in the Dominion;
or it may be the other way about.

When the Canadian statesmen were framing our
Federal Constitution they went to the United States
not for a model but for warnings. The Conference at
Quebec was held while guns were thundering on

[18] This was the case, Commissioners of Taxation vs. Baxter, Nov. 28,
1907. The discussion between the Lord Chancellor, Lord Halsbury
and the Australian lawyer is quoted by John S. Ewart in *An Imperial Court of Appeal,* Onawa, 1919. It opened with Lord Halsbury
observing "I am not aware that there is any power in this Board to dis-
regard an act of Parliament," and closed with his declaration: "I
do not know what an unconstitutional act means."

southern battlefields; in the fact of the Civil War justification was found for provisions sharply differentiating the Canadian from the American Constitution. Professor W. B. Munro in his valuable little book, *American Influences on Canadian Government,* says that Alexander Hamilton might be called "the grandfather of the Canadian Constitution." Sir John A. Macdonald, who was the chief framer of the Canadian instrument, was thoroughly acquainted with the discussions which took place over the making of the American Constitution in 1787. There is in existence his annotated copy of Madison's *Debates in the Federal Convention of 1787* with special underlinings and markings of Hamilton's draft constitution. Some of the principles offered by Hamilton and rejected by the Convention are to be found in the Canadian Constitution, among them these: Life senators; appointments by the federal government of the state governors; veto powers over state legislation by federal authority (through the governor) ; extensive powers to the central authority, exercisable for the common defense. Macdonald, forced by political conditions to forego legislative union, built a constitution which he thought fell little short of that which he desired, with the provinces having little more than municipal powers. "This," he said in his speech in the Confederation debates, "is to be one united province with the local governments and legislatures subordinate to the general government and legislature." By enlarging the powers of the central authority not only by express enactment but by allocating to it all residual powers "I am," he said, "strongly of the belief that we have, in a great measure, avoided the defects which time and events have shown to exist in the American constitution."[19] This conception of the effect of the provisions allocating the powers was emphasized by the explanations given to the British Parliament by Lord Carnavon, the Colonial Secretary, introducing the Confederation measure.

Alas for the plans of constitution makers! Professor W. P. M. Kennedy of Toronto University, whose writings on the Constitution of Canada are standard works, writing in the *Round Table* recently said that "it is doubtful if the fathers of Federation would to-day recognize their offspring." And he repeats an observation which has become a commonplace in the discussion of this matter:

We now witness on the North American continent singular political developments. The American Republic began with a theory of State rights. To-day we watch the ever-increasing growth of Federal power. Canada began its political existence with the scales heavily weighted in favor of the central authority. To-day the Canadian provinces enjoy powers greater than those of the states of the American Union. In both federations the most cherished aims of the founders have been nullified.[20]

[19] *Confederation Debates,* p. 32.
[20] See *Constitutional Issues in Canada, 1900-1931,* ed. by R. M. Dawson, London, 1933, p. 50.

This state of topsy-turvydom in Canada is the result of an attitude of mind on the part of the Judicial Committee of the Privy Council which it took up some fifty years ago and in which it persisted until a very recent date. It refused to see in the British North America Act anything but a British statute; it interpreted it by arbitrary rules of construction which excluded consideration being given to its historical origins. By this construction the powers assigned to the provinces have been given a scope which has not only swallowed up, in large part, the reserve powers of the federal government, but has actually limited the powers conferred upon the central authority. Out of the control of "property and civil rights" by the provinces was developed a theory of interpretation which has completely destroyed the balance between the Dominion and the provinces which the makers of the Constitution planned. Incidental to this great development of provincial powers, the Dominion virtually renounced the use of its power to disallow provincial legislation. Recent decisions by the Privy Council on the cases dealing with control of the radio, and the right of women to sit in the Senate, reveal a change in attitude and an inclination to recognize the need of giving the central authority all the power that can be given it under the Constitution to meet the needs of this changing world. But the damage has been done. And it is at this juncture that there has arisen in Canada a powerful and widespread demand, largely induced by recent developments in the United States, for the exercise by the Dominion of controlling powers over industry, which are far outside the bounds of its jurisdiction as fixed by judicial decisions.

There is perhaps a bare possibility that the courts might, following the precedent of the American courts, recognize an emergency right in keeping with Lord Haldane's observations in the Toronto electric case: "No doubt there may be cases arising out of some extraordinary peril to the national life of Canada, as a whole, such as the cases arising out of a war, where legislation is required of an order that passes beyond the heads of exclusive provincial competence."[21] Failing this, the situation can only be met by an amendment of the British North America Act so redistributing the legislative powers as to give the Dominion the powers that a central government requires and will require in increasing measure as time goes on. There is therefore today a loud clamor for the immediate modernization of the British North America Act. One hears on all sides and from the most unexpected quarters the question, delivered in truculent tones, whether the needs of Canada today and tomorrow are to be denied by invoking the dead yesterday. The awkward situation now emerges that while we have no domestic machinery for amending the Constitution, the procedure by which the amendment of the Constitution by the British Parliament can be invoked is not known,

[21] *Idem,* pp. 442 ff.

and is at this moment the subject of angry controversy. In view of the fact that the Constitution has
been amended at least a dozen times, this statement
sounds absurd. Yet it is the literal truth.

It is now ten years and more since in Parliament and
in the press the view began to be urged that Canada,
in anticipation of the time that could be easily foreseen when the reconstruction of our Constitution
would be required to meet the necessities of the changing conditions, should provide herself with a definitely
worked-out procedure by which changes in the British
North America Act could be initiated and carried out
with promptitude. Practical suggestions when made
looked either to the American or the Australian
model. The Dominion Parliament, it was suggested,
should enact the amendment which would become
valid when ratified by a sufficient proportion of the
provinces or by direct vote of the people as in Australia. Had this been agreed to, the British Parliament
would have been happy to transfer to the Canadian
people the power to amend the Canadian Constitution
which is now vested in it. But the proposition was resisted. Both government and opposition parties objected to the question being raised, since it touched
susceptibilities of race and religion. It was argued that
the present arrangement was satisfactory since the
British Parliament would amend the Constitution
upon request. Request by whom? This is the point
about which the controversy rages. Incidental to the

strengthening of the powers of the provinces the "compact theory" of Confederation has gained strength. This is a claim that the British North America Act is a treaty between the provinces; that in consequence it can only be changed if the governments of the nine provinces and of the Dominions are agreed; and that any province at will can veto a suggested amendment, in which case the British Parliament is estopped from making the amendment. The contention is grotesque; but it has a sufficient political backing to deter the Dominion Parliament from attempting to initiate amendments should there be provincial opposition.[22] We are therefore a country bound by an unchangeable constitution at a time when the Canadian people —like the people of other lands—are avid for change and impatient at restrictions embodying bygone ideas. Practical statesmanship is seeking to lessen the pressure, meanwhile, by working out agreed policies where powers are divided between the Dominion and the provinces and making them operative by conjoint legislation. There are cases in evidence at the moment. In order to get an ironclad law permitting control of the sale of wheat, the western provinces, by legislation, are seeking to give the Dominion Parliament power over property and civil rights to the extent necessary to carry out the agreed-upon plan.

If a critic were to say that this inability to modify

[22] For an examination of this issue, see "The Compact Theory of Confederation," by N. McL. Rogers, in *Proceedings of the Canadian Political Science Association, 1931.*

the Constitution so that it will march with the times
is a serious blemish on Canada's claim to be "an actual
democracy" the force of the challenge would have to
be admitted. If he were to say further that the admission that the British Parliament has, at least in
theory, the right to change our Constitution, and that
a British court has the last word about our laws, tends
somewhat to blemish the picture of national independence which I have drawn, I should concede the point,
pleading only that we have admittedly the right and
the power at will to remove these anomalies once we
can agree among ourselves that this should be done.
These are vestigial remnants of a past phase of our
development.

Against the assertion that Canada is a democracy
where public opinion rules and can speedily make
itself effective without having to overcome the resistance of vested interests and privilege, it could be said
that this claim is inconsistent with the fact that we
have in Canada a second chamber known as the Senate. The objection, I shall admit, is in form unanswerable; but in fact it has but little value. Our Senate, I
agree, is for a democracy an astonishing institution.
The senators are limited in number—twenty-four from
each of the four geographical divisions; the Maritimes,
Quebec, Ontario and the West. They are appointed
for life by the government of the day. They tend therefore to represent not the views of the present nor the
hopes of tomorrow but the beliefs of yesterday. It

invariably happens when a new government takes office in Canada that it is confronted by a politically hostile senate. In theory this body could bring to naught the decision of the people to bring in new men and new measures, because it claims coördinate powers with the Commons except with respect to the introduction of money bills. In practice, however, it exercises only a suspensory veto. Though there have been one or two exceptions to the rule, it does not stand out against public opinion if the latter remains constant. There have been a sufficient number of cases where its rejection of measures has been accepted by the Commons and the country to give senators a good talking point in making a defense of their institutions. There are periodical manifestations of the Senate's private conviction that it ought to play a joint part with the Commons in the government of the country—sometimes expressed in action by the rejection of bills, sometimes in talk. There is such a demonstration going forward at this moment, taking the form of speeches vigorously defending the Senate's part and threatening a larger use of its powers. The Canadian Senate is undoubtedly an anachronism in a democratic state, and its amendment is one of the problems of tomorrow.

Despite these blots on the scutcheon I make bold to say on Canada's behalf that there is no country in the world where there is a more complete acceptance of the democratic principles of government, or in which these are more thoroughly exemplified. There can be no stay of proceedings by the invocation of privilege or power based on particular rights to prevent the popular will having its way with men, with policies, or with governments. No believer in democracy, in these days of disillusionment, will say that the popular will, as formulated and applied under existing conditions, provides ideal government; but it does, with all its defects, provide the best available government for these times and, what is of supreme importance, it keeps open that road to the future in which hopes and aspirations for humanity, not now achievable, may come to fruition.

III

CANADA AS NEIGHBOR

III

CANADA AS NEIGHBOR

Peace, with Friction, for a Century

IN THE TREATY of Amity, Commerce and Navigation negotiated in 1794 between the United States and Great Britain—commonly called the Jay Treaty—its purpose is declared to be "to promote a disposition favorable to friendship and good neighborhood." On several grounds this treaty is notable. As John Bassett Moore has pointed out, it was the result of the first recourse in modern times to arbitration. Though it confirmed many of his countrymen in their belief that Jay was the most English of Americans, to his disadvantage, its suggestion that the two nations should live in amity so improved relations along the border that Americans in large numbers moved into Canada.

From New York State and Pennsylvania many thousands of families—some of them Quakers, many of them Mennonites—traveled the forest trails to Upper Canada; while in the eastern townships of Lower Canada whole townships were settled by immigrants from Vermont and New Hampshire. Racially that section of Canada became an extension of the adjoining states —most of the typical names of New England are to be found in that district to this day. This migration and the welcome given to the newcomers by the authorities were signs that the bitterness of the Revolutionary War was dying out and a "disposition favorable to friendship and good neighborhood" was taking its place. This era of good feeling withered in the atmosphere of contention which attended the dispute between the United States and Great Britain over neutral rights at sea and was completely obliterated by the War of 1812-14.

In the Anglo-American record this war is but an incident; but it has affected relations between Canada and the United States injuriously and sometimes tragically from that day to this. Canadians have never accepted the theory that this war was a by-product of the Napoleonic struggle; and their estimate of the origin of the war and the ends it was to serve is now pretty generally accepted by historians. This was a war of conquest inspired by the aggressive and ambitious believers in the "manifest destiny" of the United States who had been sent to Congress in the 1810 elections, from the states west of the Alleghenies. It was entered upon light-heartedly as being nothing more serious than a military picnic. "How pleasing," said Andrew Jackson, "the prospect that would open up to the young volunteer while performing a military promenade into a distant country." The republican standard as the result of this promenade, he predicted, was to be planted on the Heights of Abraham.[1] In the two

---

[1] Letter in the Essex Register, May 6, 1812, quoted by Keenleyside in his *Canada and the United States,* etc., p. 770.

years' war there was a succession of sanguinary encounters along the border between relatively small
bodies of men, and when hostilities ceased Canadian
soil was inviolate except for two small towns on the
Detroit River held by the Americans, against which
there were ample set-offs in the way of British occupation of United States territory. The war in the
totality of its results was a draw; the governments,
sorry and ashamed, made peace without a single reference being made to the supposed causes of the conflict.
But to the people of Upper Canada it was not a draw.
They had put into the field, in reinforcement of the
British regular forces, every man who could carry
arms; and it became a matter of proud conviction to
them and to their descendants that by their sacrifices
and their valor they had saved their country.

By the Treaty of Ghent in 1815 peace was reëstab-
lished—this is the famous and widely advertised peace
which has now endured for 120 years; but the disposition toward friendship and good neighborhood which
Jay and Grenville in 1794 sought to induce was, at
least on the part of the Canadian people, destroyed. It
is not possible to appraise the consequences, political
and economic, which have flowed from the persistence
in Canada, for more than a century, of this feeling of
latent suspicion and hostility to the United States,
which at any time could be readily stimulated into
open political activity. This feeling did not derive
solely from the resentment left by the War of 1812;

it was fed from time to time by clashes of interest and of policy between the two countries which usually had the ending which comes when iron and earthen pots collide. In speeches at international gatherings it is, I have observed, the usual thing to portray the 120 years of peace between the two nations as an idyllic period of mutual admiration and competition in concessions.

This is, of course, a fairy tale. For at least a century, first in Canada and afterwards in the Dominion, no general election was ever fought without at least an attempt being made by the Party of the Right to make political use of this anti-American sentiment. The formula was simple. In its earlier form the Party of the Left was charged with disloyal sentiments and separatist tendencies, its fell purpose being to transfer the country to the United States. The classic contest of this kind took place ninety years ago; and it injected a virus into our political life which was to affect successive generations of voters. In that struggle Sir Charles Metcalfe, the Governor-General, took the active leadership of what he called the "British party." The reformers were assailed as traitors and annexationists. The Mohawk Indians of the Bay of Quinte put the issue to the liking of the governor when they presented him with an address in which they said that "the question is simply this, whether this country is to remain under the protection and government of the Queen or to become one of the United States." Though the governor won a sweeping victory in English-speaking Upper Canada, the steadiness of the French Canadian electors nullified its effect and turned it, with no great lapse of time, into a defeat. Sir Charles went home a broken man. Lord Elgin came out to bring in the régime of limited self-government which his father-in-law, Lord Durham, had recommended. But the recollection of Sir Charles Metcalfe's success in stampeding a whole province by successful flag-waving became to political campaign managers a tradition of tactics; and as occasion offered the issue, so beautifully expressed by the Mohawks, was projected into election contests, sometimes with the deadliest effect. The outstanding instances were the reciprocity campaigns of 1891 and 1911; in both cases what looked like certain victory for the Liberals was turned into defeat by a resurgence of ultra-Imperialistic and anti-American feeling.

Yet there is the fact which may well appear amazing and incredible to older countries that in spite of occasional friction, misunderstanding, conflict of interests, and clashes of feeling, Canada and the United States have kept the peace for so long a period of time that the possibility of war between them no longer finds a place even in popular imagination. The thing to our minds in inconceivable. The traditional European policies of defense when propounded to Canadians as necessary for their security seem amazing in their absurdity. A personal illustration may be in point. Some twenty-five years ago, a young Englishman, who was then beginning a public career which carried him to heights just short of the first rank, spent some time in Winnipeg; and while there took time off to expound to me what he said were the principles which governed the foreign policy of Great Britain and all other European powers. The fundamental rule was that a country must regard every other country as a potential enemy unless it had an open or a secret understanding with it. Failing this, defensive preparations must be made. I at once applied the rule to the relations between Canada and the United States and put the problem up to him. We had no formal understanding with the United States. Should we arm against them? Should we dot the frontier with Martello towers as our grandfathers did? Should alert sentries challenge the wayfarer by night and day? The young man was game. He contented himself with saying that the rule was absolute. I am afraid I answered by saying that it was absolute nonsense. I said that the course of prudence, common sense and security for Canada was to continue to do nothing. But what if the Americans swooped down on us? In that case I said it would be a case of a head-on collision between a steam roller and a bulldog and it would be just as well, if it had to occur, that it should take place without premeditation. About the time of this conversation there appeared in England a book working out in detail a defensive plan for Canada against the United States. The sites for the forts were carefully chosen and that sort of thing. The writer was a major general of the British Army, Canadian born, a member of one of our most notable families.[2] The budding young statesman and the veteran soldier were both alike obsessed with the Old-World idea of the frontier —its perils and its responsibilities. "Frontiers," Lord Curzon once said, "are indeed the razor's edge on which hang suspended the modern issues of peace and war, of life or death, between nations." But not in North America, thank God!

There has been, I believe, a great ebbing in the strength of this hereditary anti-American feeling in the past few years; and this abatement is due chiefly to two causes. With the definite achievement by Canada of the status of nationhood, one pretext for political excitation of this feeling has been removed. The relationship between Canada and Great Britain has now been defined and accepted; in it there enter no elements of overlordship or paternalism. Our loyalties are reciprocal; they are those of kinsmen, not of master and dependent. The cry of "separatism" has thus become politically no longer profitable; if raised, as it still is tentatively, it encounters a pro-Canadian reaction powerful enough to give pause to the political engineers looking for results. Its availability for political use is thus gone; and with it has gone the twin appeal to the fear that the United States, with the

[2] *Canada and Canadian Defence,* by Major General C. W. Robinson, 1910.

connivance of Canadian politicians, might gather us in for the purpose of putting a few more stars in the American flag. Those feelings of timidity and apprehension have evaporated. There is now an almost universal acceptance of the fact that Canada has launched her ship on the great tides and currents of the world and will sail a course under her own captains, to whatever destinies lie in the inscrutable future. No man can foretell what the centuries may bring; but at this time its political absorption by the United States seems much the unlikeliest future for Canada. I use the word absorption, which has a definite meaning. This does not exclude the possibility of an understanding or even an alliance. If the world takes the road which the fates—if we may dignify the present madness of the nations with so heroic a name—seem bent on forcing it to take, something like this may indeed be necessary for the preservation of that North American civilization which is our joint possession.

The Free Interchange of Population

In this anti-American feeling to which I have referred, there was something paradoxical. There was, so to speak, nothing personal about it. The United States which threw its shadow over the lives of Canadians of a certain way of thinking was a large-looming, threatening corporate entity; but it was dissociated in the minds of those who entertained these apprehensions from the individuals who made up the entity and their business and personal activities. A typical individual of the class I have in mind might have very extensive business or personal relations with the United States; in his manner of speech, in the wearing of his clothes, in his preference for sports, in his fraternal affiliations, in his methods of business organization and operation, in his attitude, let us say, to organized labor, in his social customs he might be hardly distinguishable from the typical American of similar business and social standing. I have never known these political attitudes to stand in the way of business advantage or of personal advancement. I recall the case of a young man of some promise as an educationist, who was extremely active in saving Canada and the British Empire from the traitorous conspiracies, American-inspired, which he saw all about him. One day we missed him; and upon inquiry it was found that, having been offered a better post in the United States, he had, practically without a moment's consideration, left Canada and the Empire to their fate. His case was that of tens of thousands of others. Staying at home they would resist with great stoutness and in a mood of unchallengeable sincerity, policies of business coöperation with the United States which promised material advantage to Canada as a whole and to themselves individually; but as individuals they followed without hesitation the trail of fortune if it led south of the boundary.

To a lesser degree this was true in reverse. Americans followed their fortunes into Canada and there found themselves at home. I am speaking of course, of the earlier, freer, and happier days, and not of today when to change one's habitation from one country to the other takes on almost the importance of an international incident, with much attendant official perturbation and activity. When the land rush was in progress in Western Canada thirty or more years ago American farmers by the thousand went into that country under the lure of the prospects of cheap land, with no more sense of change than if they moved from one state to another. There was a story in Western Canada of two recent arrivals in Alberta from the United States, who proceeded from their holdings to a political meeting which they had heard was being held in a near-by hamlet. The time was 1900. A presidential campaign was going forward in the United States and a general election campaign in Canada. The meeting was an extremely lively one, the opposing candidates appearing on the same platform. The Liberal candidate was the late Frank Oliver, the Conservative R. B. Bennet, the present Prime Minister of Canada. Going home from the meeting one American settler said to the other: "Well they were sure fine speakers but could you make out who was for Bryan and who was for McKinley?" This freedom of movement went on unchecked for decades; the shuttle of life plied incessantly knitting these kindred races more closely together and building up elements of the populations which had two countries, one of birth, one of association. As was inevitable under the conditions which existed, the United States was heavily the gainer by this interchange of population. For the five last decades of the last century it is estimated that half the natural increase in the population of Canada was lost to the United States.

The United States census of 1920 showed that of living native-born Canadians one in every seven was a resident of the United States. Speaking last year to the British Commonwealth Relations Conference on the subject of Canadian-American relations I said, supporting my argument that Canada in her relationship with the other members of the Commonwealth could not ignore her North American environment, that going back a century and taking the case of a young Canadian couple just married it could be said that, as a general rule, one half their descendants would today be in the United States. I had my own family, on the paternal side, in mind when I made that statement. Later a number of Canadians who heard my remarks compared notes with me; and in every case I found my estimate under instead of over the mark. This tendency to move southward was particularly marked in families that derived in the first instance from the United States or from the original colonies. Families flowed into Canada and out again, a generation or so later. I never move about in the United States without encountering people of old

American stock who have a Canadian page, so to speak, in their family history. When I called upon the editor of a daily newspaper in one of your important cities a few years ago he told me that his family had detoured through Canada for two generations and that his father had been born in a little Canadian town in which I have myself a particular interest. An American friend of a somewhat aggressive type had a Canadian mother who was the kinswoman and bore the name of one of your great presidents. These cases could be multiplied by the million. They are not matters of no consequence; they are back of the influence that make history. The strains of common blood between the United States and Canada, the result of some five generations of a free movement of population which took little note of national boundaries or political friction, are deep and strong; and their effect on the personal, social and business relationships between the peoples of the two countries has been wide-reaching.

This free movement of population has been stopped by economic forces operating through governmental machinery. The young man from Canada seeking work in the United States these days finds the frontier barred against him; and we are equally on the alert in keeping any jobs that may be going for our own people. Immigrants to Canada from the United States last year numbered 13,196; the corresponding figure, twenty years earlier, was 139,000. There has also been, in each country, a tendency to deprive the nationals of the other country of positions they hold; this has been particularly the case in semipublic institutions like hospitals. The old easy relationship along the frontier by which people could live in one country and work in another has come to an end; along the Canadian side of the Detroit River the effect upon the towns and upon thousands of individuals has been catastrophic. The closing of the American frontier to Canadian youth has sadly restricted a Canadian industry—the equipping of young men in our universities for opportunities in the United States. An inquiry some years ago showed that 13 percent of the graduates of Canadian universities were living in the United States. A university in the Maritime provinces gave American addresses for 34 percent of its graduates. Some years ago the entire graduating class in engineering in a Canadian university found within a year occupations in the United States.

But unfortunate as these conditions may be for individuals, they represent no great diminution in the social, educational, personal and business contacts that go on between the two countries. The temporary movement of people back and forth across the boundary totals up in the course of one year, it is estimated, to 25,000,000 passages. Radio has come in to strengthen and supplement all the other agencies that tend to widen our acquaintance with one another. Interests over a wide range of activities give to radio on the

North American continent an international effectiveness unapproached elsewhere in the world. To the intelligent user of radio there is plenty of golden grain in the chaff that pollutes the air. Already the radio has become indispensable. When your outstanding political leaders take to the air they are heard in Canadian homes from the Atlantic to the Pacific. It has been of extreme value to me as a journalist to be able to follow the presidential campaign of 1932 by listening night after night to Mr. Roosevelt and Mr. Hoover and by the same means to post myself as to the "New Deal" by listening at first hand to expositions of it. The radio of course may be, and often is, an agency to repel as well as to attract, to annoy as well as to please, to excite enmity instead of encouraging amity; but on balance it must be regarded as making a considerable contribution to the cause of "friendship and good neighborhood."

The sum of all these agencies has been the development of a type of Canadian whose cousinly resemblance to conventional Americans is sufficiently marked to shock many of our worthy overseas kinsmen. Much of the misunderstanding of the years when the issue of equality was being fought out arose from a feeling, by many who hoped for a consolidated empire, that people who so resembled the Americans in their speech, their business methods, the architecture of their houses, the setting which bounded their lives, could not really be counted on to keep Canada in the

British family. The disparaging idea behind this was that Canadians were of necessity an imitative people. If therefore we were truly British, our manners, customs, and methods would have been carefully imported from England. Since that had not been done but instead there were obvious resemblances to Americans, it followed as the night the day that we were but Yankees in disguise seeking a convenient occasion for breaking up the Empire and coming out in our true colors. For years we had an unfailing procession of travelers who passed through our country, getting shocks, viewing us with alarm and posting home to issue warnings and lamentations. For my own part I got very weary of the performance; and finding myself some few years ago addressing an understanding audience in London, I exercised my right as a kinsman from overseas to speak with some frankness. Upon that occasion I said:

The Americanisation of Canada, implying ultimate absorption by the United States, becomes a profound conviction with many visitors from Great Britain after they have been in our country two or three weeks. Clergymen, bishops especially, seem particularly prone to this delusion. They come to Canada in the expectation of finding a replica of England and, when they discover the Canadian variation from English customs and standards and note their resemblance to the habits of the American people, they at once jump to the conclusion that Canada is about to be lost to the Empire, and come home to impart the sad news to the English people. Often they accompany the announcement of this startling discovery with demands that Englishmen should rush out to Canada to save the country from the Canadians and keep it on the true path of Empire.

It is the hope of some of us that we are near the end of these fears and misconceptions. The characteristics of Canada, social, political, business, linguistic, journalistic, religious, are our own affair. They are what they are because they suit us; they are integrated with the whole life of the nation; they help to produce that national whole called Canada.[3]

Economic Nationalism and Tariff Wars

It is possible that my earlier observations that anti-American feeling in Canada is lessening may have been, in some degree, misleading. What I was referring to was the national hereditary dislike born of "old far-off unhappy things and battles long ago." The Americans had their own brand of feelings of this kind. Their faith in "manifest destiny" made them impatient over the erection to their north of a country British in character and spanning the continent, which thus barred the expansion of the United States. Thus the American House of Representatives protested in 1867 against the formation of the Dominion as a violation of the Monroe Doctrine. The opinion was widely held that the Canadians really

[3] *Journal of the Royal Institute of International Affairs*, Nov., 1930.

wanted to be annexed to the United States but were in some way held back from giving effect to their wishes by British force. One of the obscure influences behind American tariff policy toward Canada was a desire to hasten what was believed to be an inevitable drift of Canadian public opinion. When the attitude veered from unyielding refusal to make any arrangement to the gracious friendliness of the Taft régime, the revelation that, in many American minds, this was just an alternative method of applying pressure, gave such body to Canadian suspicions that the one opportunity in seventy years for the making of a sensible, workable arrangement between the two countries was lost. As one who was active in the campaign for the adoption of the Taft-Fielding reciprocity arrangement, I can testify that the blows that destroyed it were delivered by its United States friends.[4] When the Speaker of the United States House of Representatives said in more than one speech, that he was for the agreement because it would hasten the day when Canada would become a part of the United States; when a United States senator spoke of annexation as "the logical conclusion of reciprocity"; when even the President of the United States made references to Canada coming to "the parting of the ways," the linked business interests of Canada which resisted

[4] The provocative statements by American politicians are reported and their effect on the reciprocity campaign estimated in J. W. Dafoe's *Clifford Sifton in Relation to His Times,* Toronto, 1931, pp. 367 ff.

the agreement for reasons which seemed good to them but which still, after twenty-three years, have to me the appearance of irrationality, were so reinforced by an outburst of traditional anti-American sentiment that the agreement was rejected and the Canadian government responsible for making it was dismissed from office. The traditional Canadian fear of the Americans the traditional American hope for northward territorial expansion, upon that occasion, came into violent collision with much resulting wreckage; but with something gained, in this important respect, that both traditions lost prestige by the outcome. Canada's contemptuous and scornful rejection of the only bona-fide friendly business offer ever made her by the United States added to American enlightenment as to Canada's fixed intentions not to be merged with the United States on any terms whatever; while we in Canada have had plenty of opportunity to reflect upon the unwisdom of permitting feelings derived from an ancient blood feud to warp our judgment in matters affecting present-day international relationships. The emergence of these particular prejudices, in anything like their former virulence and force, to hamper or destroy the efforts of our statesmen to improve relations between the two countries need not be feared.

But unfortunately it does not follow that there is now between the two North American nations perfect harmony and complete understanding with a readiness on the part of each to appreciate the other point of view and a manifest willingness to adjust difficulties.

New attitudes of mind have appeared, as intransigent as those they have displaced, though perhaps they will prove less deep-seated. The Penguin Island philosophy that neighbors are enemies still operates in the economic sphere—never so powerfully as today. If there are in the world two nations willing to trade freely with each other their whereabouts are not known to me. Willingness to trade with one another on the basis of an economic division of labor and a sharing of aptitudes and advantages is not possible even in the British family of nations. The Ottawa Conference of 1932, widely advertized as the forerunner of a family arrangement of this character was in fact a ceremony by which Great Britain introduced herself to her young relatives as a convert to their philosophy of "Ourselves first; the family next if it does not cost anything; and the outside world last of all." The young nations are not so happy as they were two years ago at the success of their large contribution to the influences that transformed Great Britain into a protectionist Britain-first country. Unless they have their heads in the sand they can see the walls in building that will shut their agricultural products out of the British market—this is what the policy of "Britain first" will mean for them. It is the opinion of a friend of mine, editorially associated with one of the great English papers, that the growth of economic nationalism in Great Britain is rapidly destroying, in the dominant Conservative party, the imperialistic sentiment which has looked forward in hope to the reconsolidation of the British Empire by something in the nature of an imperial Zollverein.

If this is how the modern doctrine of national self-containment appeals to a country like Great Britain, with its long free-trade tradition, its but slightly impaired position as a creditor nation, its obvious dependence upon export trade, what will be its harvest in the United States where it must have the appearance to many of being a world-wide confirmation of national trade policies which it has pursued, with occasional interruptions, for more than a century? To many the most puzzling feature of the world confusion of today is the universal resistance, apparently instinctive and spontaneous, by nations large and small, rich and poor, to all those influences tending to bring them closer together, influences which naturally arise from what Mr. Owen D. Young, in a contribution to the *New York Times* a few months ago, called "the compression of the world." In this article he admits that he believed, as did all people with a liberal outlook, that this compression "would be the forerunner and the issuer of a world more closely integrated in peaceful effort, in business interchange, in financial stability, in economic development, in psychological neighborliness." But the result has belied these hopes. Perhaps, Mr. Young says, "A compressed world raises barriers instead of breaking them down, nations by these means seeking to protect their individuality." Discussing this disturbing phenomenon before audiences, I have ventured an observation which I trust time will show to be based upon something more than idle hope. I have sought to find something of promise in the situation by suggesting that this is an instinctive rallying and getting together of the powers and principalities of the world of yesterday in a last desperate attempt to stave off, for another generation or so, the coming of the new world of human brotherhood and international peace; and that the violence of the reaction is the measure of the strength of the movement they seek to block.

If this is not merely the entertaining, by an effort of the will, of those "hopes undimmed for mankind" which Morley tells us it is befitting one should hold "at the close of the long struggle with ourselves and with circumstances," the hope may also be cherished that perhaps, despite the dark unpromising record of the past, these two North American nations may set the example, which the world so greatly needs, of friendliness and neighborliness by beginning to tear down tariff walls instead of adding to their frowning heights. Unless international trade is rejected *in toto* as an affliction of the human race there is now, as there has been any time these hundred years, an unanswerable case for the interchange of trade, on at least a fairly generous scale, between the United States and its neighbor to the north. It is depressing to recall that of all the attempts made in that period of time to make a trading arrangement, some ten in all, only one was a success, the short-lived Elgin-Marcy treaty which was negotiated just eighty years ago. Nor was it by a presentation of the economic argument that that success was scored, but by a cleverly insidious appeal to other motives. The report was sedulously circulated at Washington at that time that, if reciprocity was refused, the British colonies would apply for admission to the American Union as separate northern states—which was a prospect so harrowing to the slave states of the South that they saw to it that Lord Elgin's demands were met.

Trade Flows Despite Tariff Walls

In controversies in Canada over the value of the United States market to us one encounters—this was particularly true of the 1911 discussion over reciprocity—the bold claim that it is of no value because the two countries, in their relation to one another, are competitive and not complementary. The relationship is both competitive and complementary and on both counts interchange of trade is profitable. In the battling about tariffs which has been going on in the past few years one fact long hid, not only from the people generally but from such exalted persons as prime ministers, ambassadors, ministers of finance, secretaries of state—perhaps even presidents—is now almost universally accepted; and perhaps the future economic historian of these times will say that the widespread learning of this lesson was ample compensation for the defeat which the cause of freer exchange suffered, because it made possible the ultimate overthrow of the delusive idea that there is national profit in artificial trade restriction. The fact, no longer open to successful challenge, is this: that international trade is done with goods; and not with goods on one hand and something called money on the other. Even the people whom we might call "self-containers" will agree to this. Such small dribbles of international trade as they will graciously permit are to be made up of interchanges of needed goods. This being so, it follows that by so much as a country restricts imports that would otherwise flow into it because there is profit in doing so, it restricts the export of goods that would otherwise find a profitable market abroad. Therefore a country cannot increase employment at home in the aggregate by shutting out imports. The delusion that this can be done is the tap root of the tariff monstrosities to be observed in the world today. I was, for a few days, an onlooker at the Ways and Means Committee in Washington when the Hawley-Smoot tariff was in the making; every one taking part seemed to accept without question the theory that an import shut out would mean that the goods thus barred out would be produced at home with a net increase of

employment exactly equivalent to the work which
would be put into the substitute for the discarded
import. Your politicians had no monopoly of this
patent remedy for unemployment. In the Canadian
general election of 1930 it was declared on the platform and propounded in the columns of the press
that there was available for additional employment
in Canada no less a fund than $600,000,000 a year,
this being the volume of imports that, it was pointed
out, could be shut off. Knowledge of this principle
that international trade is exchange of goods and that
the employment we lose by bringing in a product is
offset by the employment we gain in the making of
the product which goes out in exchange, is now within
the intellectual consciousness of the public; but it
has not yet become operative. That is to say men do
not yet act on this knowledge. But this is a matter only
of time.

Trade relations between Canada and the United
States have been subject, in special measure, to the
handicaps of legislation embodying the economic delusion to which I have made reference. The fact that
the two countries are so alike in their resources and
their natural equipment has strengthened the popular
appeal of the delusion. We both have lumber; why
permit the exchange of lumber products? And so with
wheat, flour, coarse grains, dairy products, vegetables,
coal, and with all manufactures based upon natural
products. I have been encountering all my life the

argument that the point at which American and Canadian competition should begin is the outside markets
toward which they direct their surplus products. The
answer is written large in the history of the relations
between these two countries. "True ideas," William
James says, "are those that can be assimilated, vali-
dated, corroborated and verified." The idea that,
given a chance, trade between Canada and the United
States will expand enormously to the enrichment of
both countries, can stand all these tests—has indeed
been verifying them, in the face of difficulties, for the
last half century or more. Since the abrogation of the
Elgin-Marcy reciprocity treaty in 1866 Canadian-
American trade has been carried on by the enterprise
of business men in the face of official discouragement.
For the last forty years, less the period of the Underwood tariff, Washington has been alert and resolute
in expedients to keep Canadian imports at a minimum; and Ottawa has replied in kind. "Reciprocity
in trade or reciprocity in tariffs" was the war cry of
the Conservative Party in the "National Policy" campaign of 1878; and reciprocity of tariffs it has been.
Yet trade, searching for markets, infinitely resourceful
in seeking out channels, has succeeded, not in full
measure but in very considerable degree, in defeating
the purposes of Washington and Ottawa. The best
comment on theories that Canada and the United
States are not natural complementary trading units
is that which is made by our trade statistics. As long

ago as the fifties of the last century the trade between the United States and the British colonies multiplied itself fifteen times within three years from the coming into effect of the reciprocity treaty; and this is still the experience. Take down the fence or even lower it by a rail or two and the tide of commerce rises like a flood. Under the opportunity of the Underwood tariff, which imposed no duty, Canadian cattle entered the United States in 1920 to the number of 600,000 head. Duties imposed by the Fordney-Mc-Cumber tariff cut that number down to less than one-third within two years; but adjusting itself to the new conditions the trade climbed again by 1930 to the 200,000 mark. Then came the prohibitive rates of the Hawley-Smoot tariff: and last year a market was found in the United States for 2,107 head. There you have, in epitome, the history of tariff relations between Canada and the United States. A trade is developed by ingenious and resourceful business men until its volume excites the cupidity of powerful national interests which figure out that this market could be made useful to them; as things have been in the past it has always been easy to induce the legislators to destroy the trade thus marked down for destruction. It was only necessary to claim the market as a right, to point out the national benefit that would accrue from "keeping the money at home." A trade did not need to be large to bring the avengers of national economic integrity upon it. The ingenuity and persistence of the

successful campaign by which our poor little trade in
maple sugar was done to death some three or four
years ago, seems to me a perfect example of the tactics which have been employed over so many years
to strangle trade between the two countries.

In spite of tariff obstructions the trade between the
two countries keeps at astonishingly high levels. Canada buys much more from the United States than
from the rest of the world. The percentage figures
remain fairly constant however tariffs may change.
In 1900 (fiscal year) 59.2 percent of our imports
came from the United States. In 1913, two years after
Canada had been swept in an election by the cry that
we should have no "truck or trade with the Yankees,"
65 percent of our imports came from the United
States; in 1929, it was 68 percent; in 1932 it was 60.8
percent. We not only buy more from the United
States than from any other country but until the last
two years we sold more to the United States than to
any other country—contrary to common belief. The
comparative percentage of our exports to the United
States over a term of years ending in 1932 was over
40 percent in the case of the United States and less
than 30 percent in the United Kingdom. In the fiscal
year 1932 (ending March 31 of last year) for the
first time in many years our exports to Great Britain
exceeded those to the United States; and this will be
true to a lesser degree of the fiscal year just closed.
These percentage decreases took place on a greatly

restricted volume of trade. Now that this volume is rising it is noted that the United States is again taking first place. In both January and February of this year the United States bought more from Canada than Great Britain did; and the increase in percentages is rather startling. In January, 1934, Canadian exports to Great Britain increased over the same month last year by 39 percent, while in the case of the United States the increase was 83 percent. With an improvement in trade the old ratio will tend to reëstablish itself. With respect to our total trade the United States for a long period of years never failed until 1933 to account for more than half of it; in 1930 the percentage was 58.

Advantages of Reciprocal Trade

These statistics are full of enlightenment—particularly to Americans if they would but study them. They show that Canada supplies the United States with one of its most valuable markets. In 1929 the United States sold more goods to 10,000,000 people in Canada than to the 40,000,000 or more in Great Britain, the 70,000,000 in Germany, the 170,000,000 in Russia, the 400,000,000 in China—in fact Canada was that year the best customer of the United States in the whole world. In its trade with Canada in 1929 the United States fell short of taking payment for its exports in imports by $368,000,000, necessitating the transfer to that country of credits arising from Canadian exports to other parts of the world. It would not be unreasonable perhaps to think that the United States should have regarded the trade relations with Canada as ideal; should have gone to some trouble to preserve them and to keep so valued a customer in a friendly frame of mind.[5] But the very next year by the Hawley-Smoot tariff higher duties, many of them prohibitive, were imposed upon every Canadian export to the United States that caused inconvenience to a domestic producer. The proceeding was insensate except on the explanation that the tariff makers did not know what they were doing. They were in fact bemused by the mercantilist fallacy. They thought they could cut down the $521,000,000 of imports from Canada, the sight of which as they flowed over the already high tariff walls gave them inexpressible pain, without the outflow of $868,000,000 of exports to Canada being cut down by a dollar. Thus the already "favorable balance" of $368,000,000 perhaps would be doubled to the great advantage of the United States. The incredible shrinking of the trade between the two countries since that time is of course part of the general record of the depression; but the steady narrowing of the favorable differential between exports and imports is due directly to the United States tariff and to tariff retaliation by Canada. In the ten months of the last fiscal year for which figures are available the United States's advantage in Canadian-American trade

[5] Though Canada ceased to be the best market for United States exports, she was still in 1933 the second-best customer of the United States, with Great Britain in first and Japan in third place.

was just $30,000,000. Thus it can be seen that the Hawley-Smoot tariff back-fired.

At the moment negotiations are going on between the two countries looking to a betterment of trade relations through tariff adjustments. Being familiar with the history of the tariff relations between the two countries for the past eighty years, I have been profoundly skeptical of the possibility of any satisfactory reciprocal arrangement.[6] Speaking to an audience in Chicago seven years ago I said that it would be futile for the two countries to attempt to exchange tariff concessions. "These," I said, "are apparently impossible to obtain; and if they were obtained they would not endure beyond the moment when one party to the arrangement found, or imagined it found, that the other party enjoyed an advantage." The prospects today are brighter by just the degree of economic enlightenment that has come to the people of the two countries by their experiences of the past few years; unless this is very considerable the arrangement will be wrecked, either in the making or the ratification, by the inability of one side or both to see that the other party to the understanding must get concessions for concessions given and that these must not be recallable as soon as there is political clamor from interests that find themselves unsheltered from competition.

[6] See *Great Britain and the Dominions,* University of Chicago, Norman Wait Harris Memorial Foundation, Lectures, 1927, pp. 249 ff.

The desirability of a trade arrangement that will permit, within much freer limits, the flow of commerce is to Canada very great. More than any country in the world Canada is the result of political, not economic, forces; and the economic disharmony between its geographical divisions is too great to be adjusted by policies of national exclusiveness. Unless we can trade with the outside world our condition must be one of stagnation, with a standard of living falling to ever lower levels, and with increasing strains upon the bonds that keep our federation together. No other country, no combination of other countries can do for us, in this respect, what the United States could do to her own net profit when the balance is struck between advantage and disadvantage. The general advantage to both countries would be immeasurable; but the line-up in each country of the opposing interests and prejudices to any arrangement that may be made will be formidable. As has always been the case each country will be told that its interests have been sacrificed by incompetent negotiations and that, unless the people arise and destroy the agreement, they will be delivered to be shorn to hereditary and inveterate enemies. This has always been the line of attack; and it has never yet failed. Dealing with the recurring agitations in both countries over their tariff relations, Dr. O. D. Skelton, in his *General Economic History of Canada,* says: "It is curious to observe the persistent belief in each of the countries concerned that its case was rooted in immutable justice, but that its negotiators were as babes in the hands of the wily and unscrupulous representatives from across the border."[7] The present negotiations, if successful, will register the extent to which these hitherto invincible prejudices have lost their wrecking power; and the result may show that the economic feud which has reduced the potential wealth of North America by billions of dollars to the impoverishment of both countries is over; and that the day for intelligent, self-respecting, neighborly coöperation has begun.

This view, it might be contended, gets little support from the fate of the St. Lawrence Seaway Treaty which has just been rejected by the United States Senate. There the old cry—that the United States interests had been sacrificed to the greater shrewdness of Canadian diplomats—once again proved its power. Canadians cannot, however, find in this unfortunate circumstance anything to support a feeling of superiority; because we know that if the treaty had not been killed in the United States Senate the arguments there employed with such effect would have been heard in reverse in the Canadian Parliament. The Canadian public would have been told that the Americans had taken our negotiators into camp; that in consequence we had got much the worst of the arrangement; that the United States was securing rights of intervention

[7] *Canada and Its Provinces: a History of the Canadian People and Their Institutions by One Hundred Associates*, Adam Shortt and Arthur G. Doughty, general editors, Toronto, 1913, IX, 132.

in the control of the St. Lawrence which would destroy our sovereignty over those waters; with more nonsense of the same kind. And large numbers of Canadians would have believed all this and would have regarded the ratification of the treaty as a disaster. But prejudices hold their power by lessening margins.

Moreover the record of our diplomatic negotiations is not one of unrelieved failure. There is a considerable list of useful if minor conventions in operation between the two countries; and there has been one great and hopeful achievement which, in its usefulness and wisdom, is unique among the world's diplomatic instruments. I refer of course to the Boundary Waters Treaty of 1909 between Great Britain (on behalf of Canada) and the United States. This treaty created what is, in effect, an international court, a single homogeneous body, which for twenty-five years has been settling, without a single failure and always with complete unanimity, disputes arising over the boundary waters of the two countries.[8] The Commission, on behalf of both governments, has carried out a number of investigations into matters of the highest importance. There is also a provision by which this Commission may, by the action of both governments, be clothed with power to deal with all questions or matters of difference arising between the two

[8] See *Papers Relating to the Work of the International Joint High Commission*, Ottawa, 1929.

countries. Within the past few months I have watched this Commission at work dealing with the highly complicated question of how the waters of a boundary river should be allocated and controlled; and the technical competence of the court, the confidence and respect which it commanded from those who brought their cases before it and above all the complete absence of anything indicating that the court was made up of two national halves, vindicated the faith that self-respecting and efficient coöperation between the two countries is attainable if we can but discard those attitudes of fear, suspicion, and selfishness which have too often warped our minds. The Joint High Commission is the proof that, even under conditions as they are, these two countries can develop conjoint North American institutions; and it is a symbol of the fuller friendship and coöperation that the future will bring.

World Affairs and North American Attitudes

No discussion of Canadian-American relations would be complete without at least some reference to a development which is still below the horizon but of which there are signs visible to those who do not flinch from facing facts. This is the possibility of the emergence of a common isolationist attitude on the part of the North American nations against the outside world—North America *contra mundum,* not in an aggressive but in a defensive sense. The statesman and the student of affairs who do not realize that conditions are developing which might make this plan of possible escape from the terrors and dangers of a mad world attractive to North American minds must be keeping their eyes partly shut. Jesting talk is not always idle and I attach not a little significance to the remark which is not uncommon in gatherings, social and otherwise, where Americans and Canadians meet: the remark that since it is apparent that there is throughout the world a trend toward prewar conditions tending to certain war, the North American nations should come to an understanding to withdraw from world affairs, letting the rest of the world go to perdition at whatever rate of speed and by whatever methods seemed good to it. If the League of Nations disappears, if the collective system of keeping peace breaks down, if older nations begin to align themselves into groups keeping a precarious peace and arming themselves for inevitable war, there will be an instinctive urge on the part of the North American peoples to retire behind their ramparts and look on.

Of the natural disposition of the North American peoples to take attitudes toward outside issues, between which there are resemblances and sympathies, there have been some striking manifestations. This was first noted by me in Paris during the Peace Conference when the Covenant of the League was in the making. Upon the Commission which drafted the Covenant Canada was not represented, Lord Robert

Cecil (now Viscount Cecil) and General Smuts being in attendance on behalf of all the British Nations. But as the successive drafts of the Covenant came into the Canadian offices its provisions were subjected to critical analysis. Sir Robert Borden, the Canadian Prime Minister, prepared a memorandum in which the proposed Covenant was submitted to searching but constructive criticism designed to bring about modifications which would make it more acceptable to Canadian—and therefore to North American—opinion. The dangerous implications to Canada of Article Ten and of the articles providing for sanctions were expounded to me, as to others, by C. J. Doherty, Minister of Justice for Canada, and a member of the Canadian delegation, with a wealth of knowledge and a clarity of vision that, to my way of thinking, far outranged the somewhat similar criticisms preferred months later against the Covenant in the Senate of the United States. The Canadian delegation was alert to note and to offer resistance to suggestions that the League should have powers of control over domestic questions, such as regulation of immigration and the distribution of raw materials. At that stage the representatives of the United States at the Peace Conference were enthusiasts in their support of the provisions of the Covenant; but, as the sequel showed, the doubting, somewhat hesitant, attitude of Canada was more truly representative of North American opinion. Canada entered the League while the United States stayed out; and in the League has sought to modify the provisions about which North American opinion has been critical. Thus after some years of effort Canada succeeded in lessening the obligations imposed by Article Ten; while reluctance to give a governing body in Geneva large powers in the application of sanctions was revealed in the attitude of Canada toward the Treaty of Mutual Assistance and the Geneva Protocol.

Canada's attitude of opposition to the renewal of the Anglo-Japanese Treaty at the Imperial Conference in 1921 was equally significant in its revelation of North Americanism in Canadian foreign policy. The facts are not fully known; the episode is shrouded in obscurity. But certain statements about it can safely be made. The British government desired the treaty renewed and assumed that this would be agreed to without question by all the British nations at the Conference. When a proposal to this effect was made at the Conference it was warmly supported by Australia and New Zealand. When the Prime Minister of Canada, Mr. Meighen, declared that the treaty should not be renewed the British government was surprised and pained; and the government of Australia, through its Prime Minister, Mr. Hughes, was vociferous in its demand that Mr. Meighen's objection should be disregarded. The British government thought of the matter in the light of supposed advantage to the Empire with its varied interests all over the world. The words that Mr. Meighen used are not on record; but the burden of his case was that the preservation of good relations between the United States and the British nations was the first interest of the Empire and that these good relations would be placed in jeopardy if the treaty were renewed. Undoubtedly he suggested that there was between the United States and Canada on this question a considerable community of opinion. In the end he brought the British goverment to his way of thinking. The opportune discovery was made that the treaty did not expire for another year; and within that year the Washington Conference was held and treaties entered into which made it possible for the Anglo-Japanese Treaty to be dropped without too much laceration of Japanese susceptibilities. This is as yet the most striking illustration of North American policy, with Canada as agent, influencing world policies.

I have dealt with the possibility of the North American peoples, in the event of the collapse of the existing world structure, seeking to escape the ruinous consequences of this catastrophe by policies of withdrawal. That they could escape by these policies is highly doubtful. The world is now so small and so closely integrated that whether they like it or not the nations are members of one body. I should like to close these remarks on the note not of a foreshadowing of contingent common policies of isolation, but of policies of coöperation to the end that the catastrophe, foreseen and feared, will not arrive. There is in Canada, at least on the part of a considerable section of the people, a searching of hearts as to whether we have not made a contribution to the causes which have brought the world to its present plight by a too great insistence upon our right, under all circumstances, to retain freedom of judgment and action. There are certainly some signs of a similar stirring of conscience in elements of the population of the United States. There is in Canada beyond question a growing hope that the collective system of maintaining peace—by upholding the Covenant of the League or by the enforcement, when necessary, of the engagements of the pact of Paris—will be made effective and enduring. The Canadians who hold this hope understand that it is idle unless the maintenance of peace by collective action—which involves the application of appropriate and effective pressures to breakers of the peace pacts—becomes a ruling principle of policy for North American nations. We—I speak as one of the Canadians who cherish these hopes—believe that as our peoples come to realize that in this dwindling world there must be peace in all continents or in none, Canada will be willing to go beyond a pious expression of faith that nations which have pledged their word to abstain from war will keep their pledge of readiness to coöperate with other nations of good intent for the purpose of seeing to it that these engagements are not treated as scraps of paper. We trust that, if Canada should become of this mind, she will be the interpreter of the desires and intentions not alone of the northern half of the North American continent, but as well of her great kindred neighbor without whose coöperation Canada's sacrifice and the sacrifice of all the English-speaking peoples and of all the nations which profess the democratic faith would be fruitless. Time, destiny, her geographical position, the genius and resourcefulness of her people, her immeasurable potentialities, have made the United States of America the decisive factor in this crisis of humanity. I trust that it will not be deemed out of place if, in saying the last word in this course of lectures which I have been privileged to deliver, I should in paying tribute to your power speak also, with all respect, of your responsibilities.

INDEX

INDEX

Adams, John, his formula for empire (1774), 20

Alaskan boundary dispute, 69 ff.

American influences in Canada: references to, by Lord Durham, 52; fear of U.S. prime factor in bringing about confederation, 59 ff.; in extending area of Dominion to Pacific, 61 ff.

American Revolution, 15, 17, 19, 23, 24

Anglo-Japanese Treaty, 125

Annexation: as a subject of political discussion, 47; manifesto of 1849, 53; suggestions by U.S. public men after Civil War, 61; exploited for political purposes, 92, 93, 105

Australia, 16, 17, 74

Aylesworth, Sir A. B., 70

Baker, Philip Noel, 9n

Baldwin, Robert, 48, 50

Balfour declaration (1926), 22

Beer, George L., *The English-Speaking Peoples*, 4

Bidwell, M. S., 48

Blake, Edward, 37

Borden, Sir Robert, 38n, 124

Boundary Waters Treaty (1909), 121

British Commonwealth Relations Conference (1933), 7

British Empire: First Empire, 13, 21, 23; Second Empire, 24, 26, 30; transformation into a commonwealth by concession of equality to the Dominions, 38, 39, 68

British North America Act: enacted by Imperial Parliament, 61; as affected by judicial interpretation, 79; proposed amendment of, 80; controversy as to methods of amendment, 82

Brown, George, 59, 60n, 65

Bryce, James Bryce, Viscount, *Modern Democracies*, 75

Canada: provinces of Upper and Lower Canada created, 26; union of Upper and Lower Canada, 36, 37; Dominion of Canada created, 61 ff.

Canada and the United States: common origin of early colonists, 11; common customs and institutions, 12, 31, 33, 44; parallels in Canadian and American history, 19 ff.; immigration and emigration, 25, 45, 46, 89, 97 ff.; political influence of American immigrants, 47, 49; Durham's proposals to check American influence, 51 ff.; Canadian fears of American aggression and confederation, 57 ff.; diplomatic relations, 64 ff., 71, 72, 120; Alaskan boundary dispute, 69 ff.; Amer-